MATCH
OF MY LIFE

MATCH
OF MY LIFE

Eleven stars relive their greatest games

Sussex CCC

Bruce Talbot

This edition first published by Pitch Publishing 2012

Pitch Publishing
A2 Yeoman Gate
Yeoman Way
Durrington
BN13 3QZ
www.pitchpublishing.co.uk

A CIP catalogue record is available for this book from the
British Library

ISBN 978-1-908051-79-0

Typesetting and origination by Pitch Publishing.

Printed in Great Britain by TJ International.

Acknowledgements

AFTER WRITING TWO books on Sussex, which were fortunately well received, with my friend and press box colleague Paul Weaver, it was slightly daunting to go solo on this project.

It has been made a lot easier thanks to the support of a lot of people connected with Sussex cricket, not least some of the subjects who re-tell their stories of some of the great games in the county's history.

Whittling down the number of great matches since Sussex was founded back in 1839 down to 11 was not easy. I could easily have chosen 111 and it would have been just as straightforward to pick 11 from the last ten years, the most successful decade in the club's history.

But there is so much more to Sussex cricket, of course, than the years since 2003. I would argue that no county club has produced such an abundance of talented and above all interesting characters, never mind their achievements on the field.

For help in pointing me in the direction of some of the more interesting games from Sussex's past I must thank

Roger Packham, who knows as much about the county's history as anyone. Roger also proof-read the text and spotted my howlers. If any have escaped the net then it is entirely my fault. He was generous with his time and encouragement and without him the project would not have got off the ground.

Rob Boddie, Sussex's venerable archivist, was happy for me to plunder the club's vast collection of books, photographs, scorecards and newspaper clippings for research purposes and my thanks go to him and everyone at the club who has supported and encouraged this book.

My main appreciation, of course, go to the players themselves, well at least those who are still around to be interviewed! Jim Parks was a great interviewee on two counts: his memory of the first one-day final at Lord's was pin-sharp and he also leant some colour to the chapter about the last game before the outbreak of the Second World War at Hove, when Jim watched as a young boy as Hedley Verity skittled Sussex during his father's benefit game.

It hasn't always been glory for Sussex of course. Who can ever forget the NatWest final defeat to Warwickshire in 1993? Neil Lenham happily stopped selling cricket bats and pads in the Newbery shop to talk me through that day and the extraordinary week which preceded it.

Ian Gould is a less frequent visitor to Hove than he would like to be now he travels the globe as one of the ICC's elite panel umpires. Fortunately, he spared the time to reminisce in his own unique style about the 1986 Lord's triumph when "Gunner" and his boys stole Clive Lloyd's thunder.

Of course the success of the last decade had to be chronicled but in going back over the famous triumphs I managed to get some enjoyable and interesting new perspective on the successes of 2003, 2006, 2007 and 2009. It was great to catch up again with Chris Adams, Murray Goodwin, Mushtaq Ahmed, James Kirtley and Jason Lewry, a quintet whose performances on the pitch shaped that unprecedented era of success and, like all of us who witnessed them, were happy to reminisce about the part they played.

I also enormous thanks to Chris Waters, who took time from promoting his own outstanding book on Fred Trueman, to do some more research on the 1939 game against Yorkshire and other press-box colleagues for their encouragement and help, in particular John Barnett, Mark Baldwin and Paul Weaver, who looked over the text and offered some sagacious advice. Simon Dack sourced many of the photographs – most of which he took himself!

The project would never have got off the ground had it not been for the encouragement of Paul and Jane Camillin at Pitch Publishing and I trust they are as pleased with the finished product as I am.

Finally, much love as always to my wife Alison and daughter Millie for their continued love, support and patience when I disappeared "to do a couple of hours on the book".

Bruce Talbot, October 2012

CONTENTS

JASON LEWRY

2003: Worth the Wait

THESE DAYS, WHEN even a single change to the England Test team is headline news, and players can often play in 15 Tests in a calendar year without a break, tap-room (or, in Hove's case the Jim Parks' Bar) tittle-tattle will occasionally turn to the one-cap wonders, those players who were chosen for a Test on the basis of county form and quietly discarded when the selectors realised that they weren't good enough.

Sussex have had their fair share including two former captains, Paul Parker and Alan Wells. Jason Lewry never even got that far. An A tour to Zimbabwe in 1997, when a homesick Lewry couldn't wait to get back home to Worthing, was the closest he got to the England 'bubble'.

It should have been a lot different. Ask any of his contemporaries in the Sussex side – and many an opponent – and his name always comes up in conversations about players who were deserved of England recognition at the highest level but never got it.

Chris Adams, who threw Lewry the new ball in Championship cricket for most of his 11 years as Sussex captain, is unequivocal. "Jase was one of the most naturally talented bowlers I had the privilege of playing with," he said. "He could do things with the new ball that few players of his generation could. When you think of some of the bowlers who did play for England during his time in the game it is staggering that Jason never got further than an A tour. He was an outstanding new-ball bowler."

Mushtaq Ahmed agrees: "More often than not Jason and James Kirtley would get wickets with the new ball for us, sometimes two or three. And that meant that when I came on it was against players with less knowledge of how to play leg spin. He was a wonderful bowler and he should have played for England, definitely."

Instead, Lewry had to settle for being one of the most garlanded of the all-conquering team Adams led during the first decade of the 21st century. He has three Championship winners' medals and although his one-day appearances for the county were much more sporadic there is certainly no hard feeling on his part at missing out on memorable days at Lord's, Trent Bridge and Edgbaston. Indeed, as someone who suffered from injuries, including a stress fracture of the back, not playing much one-day cricket probably added two or three years to his career.

Three years after retiring in 2009 Lewry is happy to reflect on his part in a wonderful era for Sussex and in particular his memorable cameo in the game against Leicestershire in 2003 when, glory be, Sussex won the Championship for the first time in their history.

The freshest memories of that unforgettable occasion for those who were there are undoubtedly Murray Goodwin's title-clinching boundary off Phil DeFreitas and Mushtaq's

100th wicket of the season on the first day when, finally, Sussex supporters began to realise that history was going to be made in front of them.

Lewry's contribution in that game tends to be overlooked when rheumy-eyed Sussex supporters begin their reminiscences of those golden September days a decade ago, but on the third day Lewry ran through Leicestershire with eight second-innings wickets for 106. His team-mates were eternally grateful when Lewry, as was his wont, began to swing the old ball prodigiously and started to skittle Leicestershire wickets like nine-pins. That third day's play had become something of a distraction to a party which had begun straight after the title had been clinched the previous evening and which was to continue for the next few weeks.

"How Lewry managed to take eight wickets that afternoon is something I don't even think he could fathom out," says his captain. "But we are glad he did. Most of us were still hung over when we walked down the steps that morning and Jason was certainly one of them!"

The end of the longest journey had become the start of the longest night when the players retired to the *Sussex Cricketer* pub on the Thursday evening, shortly after Murray Goodwin had walked off to one of many standing ovations that day with 335 runs to his name and the title won.

There was a ruthless professionalism to the squad of 2003. They wouldn't have won the title otherwise and a few days earlier Lewry had been on the end of a fearful rollocking from coach Peter Moores in the aftermath of an innings defeat at Old Trafford in the penultimate game against Lancashire which had threatened to derail the quest for glory.

"Losing that game was a massive disappointment," Lewry recalls. "There was rain around on the second and third days when we lost half a day's play and I think we thought there wasn't enough time left in the game for us to lose. But we got rolled in the first dig and lost by an innings. A few of the lads went out that night for a couple of drinks – nothing major because we had a one-day game the following day – but I was asleep by 8.30pm.

"Next day I must have looked awful because Mooresy gave me a proper dressing-down in the huddle before the game and he humiliated me in front of the others. I spoke to him later and told him I hadn't gone out and he said he knew but just needed to say something and I was the unfortunate person on the end of it! It worked though. We beat them easily in the one-dayer by nine wickets, when Lancashire needed to win to get promotion in the National League, and we travelled home before the Leicestershire game feeling a lot better about ourselves."

* * * * *

As he sat in a semi-circle with his team-mates a few hours after Leicestershire had been beaten, sipping a beer and contemplating what they had just achieved, Lewry reflected on how quickly his fortunes had changed. A year earlier, after Sussex had fought hard all summer just to stay in Division One after promotion, he even contemplated retirement. His confidence was shot after a season plagued by knee trouble which restricted him to ten Championship games and a modest 33 wickets. "I was desperately short of confidence at the end of 2002," he reflects. "I was bowling away-swingers round the wicket and basically wondering what I was doing."

As much as making sure his body was right, Moores spent the following winter rebuilding Lewry's occasionally fragile confidence. "Jase was one of the most naturally talented players I ever worked with but he didn't always have that self-belief that top sportsmen need. When he turned up in 1994 from club cricket at Goring we took a bit of a punt on him. He'd taken shed-loads of wickets but he didn't even have a proper run-up, he just ran up off four or five paces. But he had that precious ability to swing the ball. And throughout his career sometimes he needed to be reminded, in a subtle way often, just how good he could be."

His body often betrayed him. The stress fracture was potentially career-threatening although he made a full recovery but by 2003 it was creaky knees which were causing him most concern. Pre-season fitness work was getting more difficult. It had become something of a ritual when I talked to him ahead of the season that it might be his last.

It didn't take long, though, for Lewry to witness something which he thought might prolong his career and ease his workload. It wasn't a miracle cure for his various stresses and strains – in 2003 it was a thigh strain which kept him out for five games – but the arrival at Hove of Mushtaq Ahmed, someone who would quite happily bowl all day or at least tie one end up and allow the seamers – Lewry, James Kirtley, Robin Martin-Jenkins, Billy Taylor and Paul Hutchison – to rotate at the other end.

"When Mushy signed it changed the way we bowled as a team completely," he says. "He was a godsend to the rest of us and definitely prolonged my career. Mooresy realised my strengths were as a four-day cricketer and rarely used me in one-day cricket unless there were injuries or someone was badly out of form. So when I did play I was usually fit and relatively fresh and then during games themselves I'd take the new ball and then would come back if it started to reverse, but I never had to bowl really long spells because Mushy would quite happily do that.

"I remember his debut came against Cardiff UCCE at Hove at the end of April. It was cold and he wasn't long off the plane but he took 11 wickets and they were mesmerized by him. Okay, they were students, but as the season began, and even though he needed a couple of games to get going, you could see that a lot of guys on the circuit who had been around a long time didn't really have a clue how to play him."

While Mushtaq was soon among the wickets, Lewry struggled for form. In the first seven Championship games – two of which he missed because of the thigh problem – he took a modest 13 wickets. Then it all came good at Arundel, his favourite ground not least because it was only a ten-minute drive from home.

Sussex went into the game against Essex having won four and lost three. They were six points behind Surrey and 12 in front of Lancashire, who had played a game less.

The first three days were hard-fought. Lewry, on the ground where he had made his Championship debut nine years earlier, took five first-innings wickets and Tony Cottey made his second successive hundred. But Essex began the final day leading by 235 with four wickets in hand.

"Grizz announced before play that we probably needed to take those wickets in the first 40 minutes to have a chance. It was sunny, bone dry and the ball was reversing and I remember having it under lovely control that Saturday morning."

Lewry took 3-8 in 35 balls to complete match figures of 10-124, his best for two years. Sussex needed 256 in 82 overs but were 32-3 when Cottey and Tim Ambrose came together. Cottey made 98 and Ambrose an undefeated 93 and Sussex won by six wickets with 4.1 overs to spare. "It was real cat-and-mouse stuff," says Lewry. "Cotts hadn't had the best of times with us before 2003 but he proved his worth that season."

Cottey made another hundred a few days later as Sussex won at bottom of the table Leicestershire to trim Surrey's lead to five points. But Lewry bowled just six overs before succumbing to a side strain which sidelined him for the next three matches against Nottinghamshire, Surrey and Lancashire. Sussex drew the first two but then defeated Lancashire by 252 runs when Adams scored centuries in both innings and victory was wrapped up with just 12 minutes to spare, Mushtaq taking 5-23 in 17.2 overs in a memorable final session.

The gap between Surrey and Sussex was down to five points as Lewry returned for the trip to Castle Park, Colchester to make a telling contribution against Essex – with the bat. On the first day Sussex piled up 521-8 with Goodwin scoring a double hundred. Matt Prior smashed a century after tea as Lewry admired the audacity of the 21-year-old's stroke-play from the other end. The next morning Lewry joined in the fun with 70 – his maiden first-class half-century and the third career-best of the Sussex innings. They were eventually bowled out for 612.

Lewry took one wicket and bowled 20 overs in the match, sharing the new ball with Billy Taylor as James Kirtley went off to launch his England Test career. Predictably, as Essex were forced to follow on 329 behind, Mushtaq finished with seven wickets.

"Funnily enough, some of the Essex batsmen played Mushy as well as anyone," says Lewry. "Andy Flower was a great player of spin, Nasser Hussain got 95 against him at Arundel which was a fantastic duel and Ronnie Irani also got after him. At Colchester Billy stepped up although by then, and with James off playing for England, we basically just dovetailed around our kingpin."

Sussex's next game was at home to Middlesex and Lewry made a decision which he still regrets ten years later. "People sometimes questioned my attitude but I missed my younger brother Damien's wedding to play in that game," he says. "At the start of the season when I knew the date I didn't think it would be an issue. He was getting married on the Saturday and the game started the previous day. Mooresy left the decision to me and because of what was at stake I decided to play and I ended up missing the wedding. I still regret that. At the time I felt I was doing the right thing but looking back it was probably very insensitive of me."

In Lewry's defence, Kirtley's continued absence left Sussex short of a new-ball bowler but after Middlesex, who won the toss, had made 392 thanks to hundreds from Andrew Strauss and Owais Shah Sussex found themselves 107-6 just about the time Damien Lewry was tying the knot.

Then came one of the great Sussex fightbacks. Off-spinner Mark Davis, often a peripheral figure that season because of Mushtaq, came out of the shadows to put on 195 for the seventh wicket with Matt Prior, who scored 25 boundaries in a magnificent 148. Davis carried on during the third morning before holing out for 168 while Mushtaq made a half-century,

Taylor a career-best 35 not out and Lewry 21. The last four wickets had put on 430 runs.

"That was probably the period in the season when we thought we would win the title," says Lewry. "We were in a desperate position but Mark Davis was a very capable batsman and Mooresy kept telling anyone who would listen that at some stage during the season he would help us out. I was feeling terrible because I hadn't gone to Damien's wedding but then Matty and Mark started to take the game away from them. We got a few more the next day and with Mushy in the side we always fancied our chances of bowling them out again in their second innings."

Lewry bowled 25 overs in the second innings and took three wickets, including Strauss. Mushtaq, having gone wicket-less for 26 overs, finished with four wickets and ten in the match for the fifth time in the season. He now had 99 for the summer.

Mushtaq was by now struggling with various aches and pains as the sheer physical toll of bowling so many overs, often in high-pressure situations, began to take their toll. Lewry recalls: "Mushy seemed to age quite a lot as the season wore on but by then he was at a stage taking the ball out of his hand, even if it was for a change of ends, was difficult for Grizz.

"As a bowler I knew how much physical strain he was under and if it had been me I wouldn't have captained him that way. But he just loved bowling and, looking back, Mooresy and Grizz handled him pretty well. At times they would put their point across and he would do the same but eventually Mushy kind of got his way. Seriously, some days I think he would happily have bowled all day from both ends if he could. He just loved the challenge. He was quite happy if me or James or

Billy knocked over the top two or three. Sometimes he would open the bowling but it wasn't so easy for him to bowl with a hard ball. The game-plan was to let him loose at the middle order and sit back and watch it happen."

Having dismissed Middlesex for 250, Sussex sped to their target of 106 in 97 minutes and travelled to Old Trafford the following day with an 18-point lead over Surrey, who had played a game more. Lancashire were now the only side who could deny them but ten points from the penultimate game would secure the title.

"It was strange because from early in the week the forecast up there was for rain so we knew that there would probably be less time to get a result," says Lewry. "I think a lot of people thought we would win it up there. I remember a lot of our sponsors and supporters travelled up on the Friday expecting a party the next day but it didn't happen."

Lancashire were desperate to avenge their defeat at Hove a few weeks earlier. Their players and management felt Mushtaq's excessive appealing had contributed to some of his dismissals on the final day and prepared a green, seaming pitch tailor-made for their own attack which would also negate Mushtaq's influence.

The rain did come. On the first two days 77 overs were lost but there was a timidity to Sussex's approach. Kirtley, fresh from a successful England debut, had sore shins and was badly missed as Stuart Law won a compelling duel with Mushtaq to score a hundred. So did Mal Loye and Sussex could only claim two bonus bowling points while Mushtaq bowled a fruitless 37 overs in search of his 100th wicket.

Lancashire declared on the third morning on 450-6 before the burly John Wood blew a hole in Sussex's batting with three wickets in nine balls. Murray Goodwin, felled by Peter Martin's bouncer and forced to have stitches inserted above his eye, carried his bat for 118 but Sussex had to follow on 199 runs behind and were bowled out for 180 in their second innings. Left-arm spinner Gary Keedy finished with ten wickets and declared: "We gave them a good hiding."

"We learned that week that you can never play a game around the weather," says Lewry. "Lancashire thought we were a one-man team and they were hell-bent on beating us. Our mind-set was totally wrong. In a way we were fortunate because losing to them didn't really affect our position at all. We knew what we had to do going into the Leicestershire game which was get six points. But we were taught a big lesson in that match."

Wednesday 17th September dawned bright and sunny – the perfect late-summer English day. But as he drove to the ground Lewry couldn't quite believe what he was seeing as a long crowd of spectators snaked down Eaton Road. A queue to get in to a Championship game? That was a first.

"There were quite a lot of nerves around, even among guys who had played a lot of cricket," says Lewry. "By the time we started the ground was pretty much full, there were TV cameras everywhere and lots of press. The atmosphere did feel different. I think people expected us to win the Championship now."

In truth, Sussex supporters who had waited a long time for this moment were as tense as the participants. True, there was no one in the ground who had waited 164 years since the club's formation but there were plenty who had been there on the six occasions since 1968 when Sussex finished stone-cold last, most recently 2000.

Leicestershire, already relegated and giving a debut to their teenage all-rounder Luke Wright, were thought to be compliant opponents but there was an audible groan around the County Ground when it was announced that they had won the toss and would bat first. Sussex were unchanged. "We knew what we needed to do first which was bowl them out, then we would re-assess," says Lewry. "We had a chat in the middle and all the talk was about taking it session by session."

Leicestershire lost opener John Maunders with the score on 42 but their two best batsmen, Darren Maddy and the Australian Brad Hodge, looked relatively untroubled until a moment that was as memorable to those who witnessed it as the clinching of the title the following day. In the last over before lunch Hodge played forward to a leg break and lost his off stump. Mushtaq had his 100th wicket and the ball with which he took it would later be mounted and presented to him.

"It was a massive relief to Mushy and the whole team when he got his 100th," says Lewry. "It changed the whole mood really." Leicestershire collapsed after lunch and were all out for 179 in the 70th over. Three bowling points gained, all Sussex needed to make sure of the title was to score 300 in their first innings and claim three batting points. They made careful progress throughout the rest of the first day and closed on 137-1, another 163 still needed.

Fourteen more runs were added on Thursday morning when Tony Cottey was out for 56 and Adams walked out to join Goodwin.

"We'd had a huddle and Murray made the announcement that he wanted to be the person who got the 300th run and our third point," says Lewry. "As it got closer and people knew we were going to do it and that those two would be there when we reached 300 it would have been appropriate if Grizz had got the winning run but Muz was quite determined.

"They always had an interesting relationship. There was a lot of rivalry but also plenty of mutual respect. They were different individuals and if they met in the street I'm not sure they would have got on but it worked well. They always batted well together."

The moment it seemed the whole of Sussex had been waiting for finally arrived at 1.43pm. Goodwin spotted a short ball from Phil DeFreitas, rocked back and pulled it to the mid-wicket boundary. Sussex had 300, six bonus points and, after 164 years of trying, their first County Championship.

"Since lunch we knew it was coming, it was just a matter of when," says Lewry, who was stood arm-in-arm with his team-mates and the coaching staff on the balcony when Goodwin hit the winning runs. Adams leapt into the air and the pair embraced.

Unbeknown to Lewry and the players, Sussex president Jim Parks had spoken to the umpires at lunch and arranged for the game to be stopped. The squad tumbled down the balcony steps to join Goodwin and Adams on a lap of honour while the Tannoy blared out that old county anthem 'Sussex by the Sea'.

While the Leicestershire players sat somewhat bemused on the outfield the squad walked slowly around the boundary edge soaking up the applause and adulation of the crowd. Eventually, after eight minutes, umpires Trevor Jesty and Mervyn Kitchen decided they had better get on with the game.

"The lap of honour just sort of happened but it was a wonderful moment," says Lewry. "We kept looking and thought someone would say something, but it was just accepted and all these supporters that had been watching Sussex for years were beckoning us to the boundary edge. A lot of people were holding back tears, others couldn't do it and it brought home just what we had achieved and what it meant to so many people. I'm quite a reserved sort of bloke, but when I came back up the steps to the dressing room I was struggling to stop the tears."

While Goodwin batted on and on to a new county record for the highest individual score and Adams added to the party atmosphere with a century of his own, the dressing room became open house for all manner of well-wishers including family members, sponsors, club officials and even one or two fortunate members of the media. And it wasn't long before plans were being made to continue the celebrations, so far limited to a sip of warm champagne, long into the night.

It wasn't just the players in the mood to party. Goodwin walked off with 335 to his name and Sussex declared on 614-4 as soon as he had broken Duleepsinhji's record. Lewry took another wicket with the new ball as Leicestershire reached 38-2 at stumps.

A few minutes later the Sussex Cricketer pub at the entrance to the ground was packed with revellers. It seemed the natural place for the players and coaching staff to begin their own celebrations in earnest.

"Everyone was in there and I mean everyone who had anything to do with Sussex cricket," says Lewry. "The atmosphere was wonderful and of course people would start filling your glass as soon as you'd finished your drink. I could hold my beer back then. I could drink a decent amount and still be okay the next morning but not that night. I had arranged to stay with Ian Poysden, one of our sponsors, and I remember getting in at about 5am, collapsing in the bed in their spare room and being woken what seemed like ten minutes later by Ian's wife Michelle at 8.30am.

"She drove me to the ground in my suit and I remember stumbling out of the car and immediately falling flat on my face on the pavement outside the ground. I hobbled into the ground with blood all over my knee and looking very much worse for wear."

He wasn't the only one.

"Mushy was okay because he didn't drink of course but everyone else was in a state of dishevelment. Grizz was so bad he didn't lead us out so James Kirtley, who was 12th man because he still hadn't got over his injury, led us out and had to nip off to the hospitality boxes to be sick.

"But the thing I most remember about that morning was when an old lady walked into the ground pushing a shopping trolley and just walked across the pitch. I had never seen anything like it. Not many people remember that because of what else happened over those three days but for some reason it's one of my biggest memories of that game."

With Mushtaq worn out and sitting in the dressing room Adams knew taking the remaining eight wickets might take some time so he struck a bet with Lewry. "He was standing at mid-off and said if I took a wicket he would run around the outfield naked that night. I got a wicket and then another and that night he ended up doing about three circuits of the outfield. It was pretty dark so I don't think too many people in the flats around the ground noticed and they would probably have forgiven him anyway!"

Suddenly, as the old ball began to reverse, Lewry got his second wind. Leicestershire had taken the score to 277-4 thanks to a hundred by John Sadler and it looked as if they would at least take the game to a fourth day. Billy Taylor made the breach after night-watchman David Masters had made his maiden century while Lewry got to work with five wickets for six runs in 25 balls. "I still felt pretty rough although the worst of the hangover had worn off by then," says Lewry. "It was after tea and once I got a couple of wickets I thought how good it would be if we could get this over and done with now so we could basically start partying again."

When Lewry wrapped up the Leicestershire innings by having former Sussex player Vasbert Drakes caught behind for a duck he had taken 8-106 – career best figures – and Sussex had eased to their tenth win out of 16 by an innings and 55 runs. Their winning margin ahead of Lancashire was 34 points. No other county won more than six games.

A few moments after Lewry led the team off to the umpteenth standing ovation of the game the players were back out on the balcony while thousands of fans swarmed onto the outfield to watch the celebration. It was a full two hours before the last of them had reluctantly left. If you had told them that this was not some glorious one-off but the first of three Championships in the space of four years they would have laughed heartily and raised another glass in celebration.

As dusk settled the players made their way onto the square for their own private reflections on what they had achieved. "That was a great moment," says Lewry. "We were all asked one by one what the highlight of the season had been and

I just said this. Who would have thought at the start of the season we would be enjoying a moment like that."

More partying followed. "We went out that night and then again and then there was an open-top bus parade and civic reception," continued Lewry. "Basically, I wore the same suit I turned up in on the second day for the next four days and my car didn't leave the ground for about three weeks. But it was a wonderful time."

At the house in Ford, near Arundel, he shares with his wife and four children there isn't much room for memorabilia. He has the ball which he took eight wickets with somewhere and there's the shirt he wore framed and some pictures taken on the balcony when the post-presentation celebrations were in full swing. Now and then he will get out the marvellous dvd of that season produced by Sussex and watch it with his twin boys.

Lewry played in Sussex's other two Championship wins in 2006 and 2007 but nothing will beat the first time. "2006 was strange because we won it away from home and 2007 was pretty awful in a way because we waited around all afternoon wondering if Lancashire might snatch it from us," he says.

"For me nothing will surpass 2003. I had been at Sussex since 1994 and there had been some very tough years before we won the Championship. I probably bowled better in quite a few games that season than I did against Leicestershire and anyway no one's going to remember what I did? Mushy got his 100th wicket and Murray scored 335. But I will never forget it."

Neither will those privileged enough to be there.

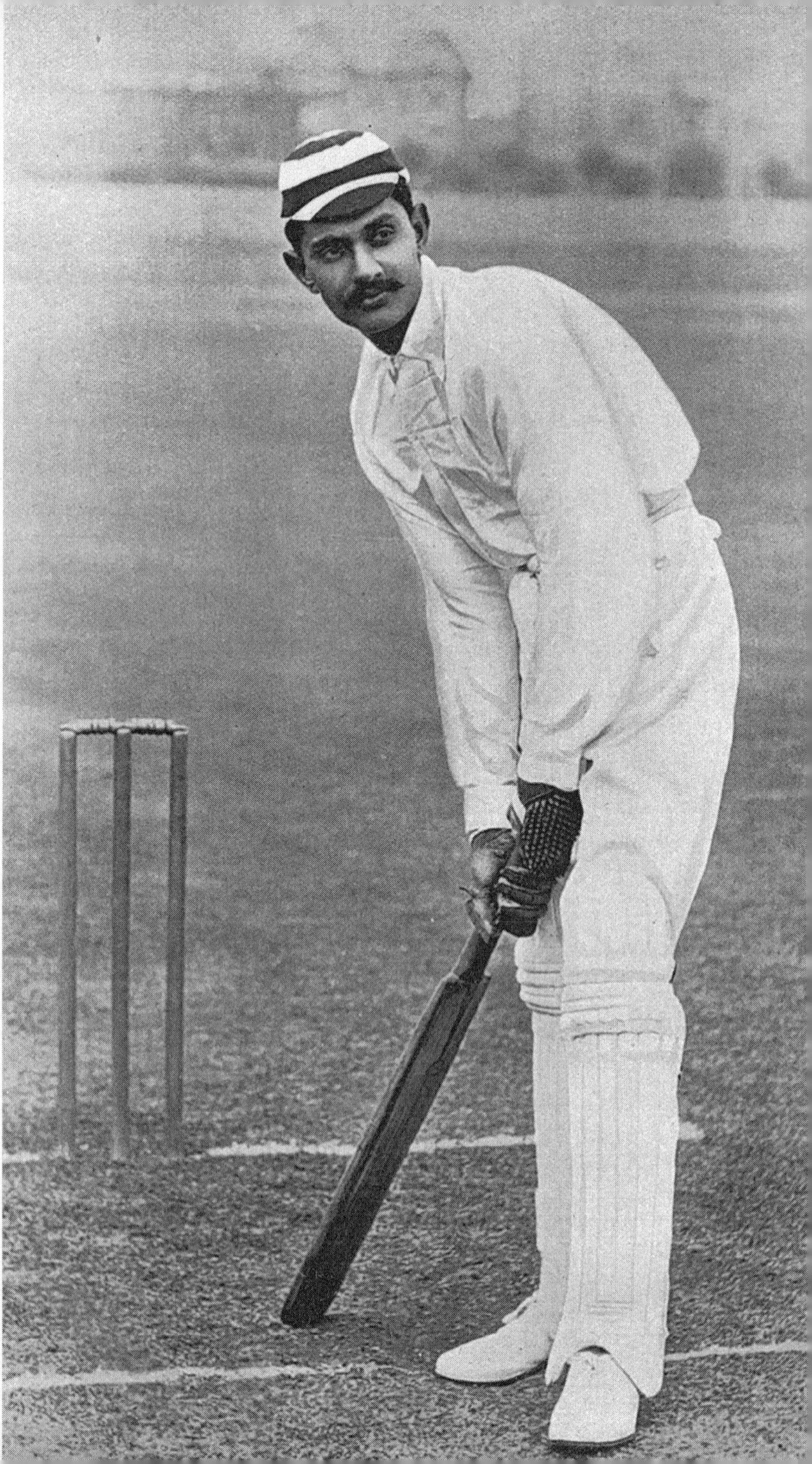

KUMAR SHRI RANJITSINHJI

1896: A Prince in his Prime

KUMAR SHRI RANJITSINHJI was cricket's first global superstar. During cricket's Golden Age at the end of the 19th century "Ranji" was arguably the most talented and certainly the most exotic cricketer in an period of brilliantly accomplished and flamboyant players. His peers – Sussex team-mate CB Fry, Gilbert Jessop and even the great WG Grace – acknowledged it and so did his adoring public, both in his adopted county and beyond at a time when Test and county cricket was firmly establishing itself in the nation's consciousness thanks to the growth of the popular press.

Ranji was more than just a fine cricketer, credited with the invention of the late cut and leg glance. But how could you compare him with the current generation of players? Well, think of a player with the wristy skills and dexterity of Sachin Tendulkar with the peacock's showmanship of a Kevin Pietersen. Even then you don't come close to describing a player of his extraordinary gifts.

"From the moment he stepped out of the pavilion he drew all eyes and held them," wrote Jessop in the 1920s. "No one who ever saw him bat will forget it. He was the first man I know who wore silk shirts, and there was something very romantic about the very flow of his sleeves and the curve of his shoulders. He drew the crowds wherever he went, and at the height of his cricket days the shops in Brighton would empty if he passed along the street. Everyone wanted to see him. Whenever I bowled against him I felt he was impregnable. My impression was 'I will never get this man out'. He was indisputably the greatest genius cricket has ever produced."

A century and more on some might question the validity of Jessop's statement but at the turn of the 20th century Ranji became the first sportsman, and certainly the first non-white sportsman, in the world to gain renown and respect beyond the boundaries of the game they played.

Sussex historian Home Gordon wrote: "Old gentlemen waxing plethoric declared that if England could not win without resorting to the assistance of Asiatic extraction it had better devote its skill to marbles. One MCC veteran told me that if it were possible he would have expelled me from the club for having the disgusting degeneracy to praise a dirty black." Scores of 62 and 154 not out at Old Trafford on his England debut in 1896 only partially placated his critics.

MCC had little choice but to select him. His achievements at the time were known not only to cricket followers but to those who took merely a passing interest in the game. In 1896 he scored 2,780 runs – a new record – including ten centuries. In 1899 he made 3,159 runs and 3,065 the following year which included five double-centuries, an astonishing performance given that no one had scored more than two in a season up until then.

And at the height of his powers Ranji achieved something that has never happened again in the history of the game – against eventual county champions Yorkshire in August 1896 he scored two hundreds in the same day.

Born in 1872, he had been brought to England in 1888 by the principal of his Indian college to study at Trinity College, Cambridge. It soon became apparent that he had little regard for academic studies, preferring instead to play games. As well as cricket, he was a superb racquets player thanks to his astonishingly powerful eyesight. "I played often with him and against him and it seemed his eye was infallible," wrote Jessop. He could judge the length or flight of the ball so quickly that he had time then to decide which shot to play."

Ranji had played cricket in India but it was while watching Australia's CTB Turner take a hundred off the Surrey attack at the Oval during that first summer in England in 1888 that he decided to devote his energies to the game. He was a magnificent batsman with so many natural gifts but he practiced assiduously when the Surrey professionals went to work with the Cambridge students to hone his talent.

It was around this time that he perfected the leg glance, initially by anchoring his right leg to the ground during practised. He would move his left leg away from the ball towards the covers and discovered in doing so that he could turn or flick the ball behind his legs. The shot had probably been played before but not with the same effectiveness.

Ranji's prolific run-scoring in games around Cambridge began to get him noticed and by 1895 he had become friendly with the amateurs in the Sussex team and in particular CB Fry, who was studying at Oxford and against whom he had occasionally played, as well as the county captain Billy

Murdoch, who was keen for Ranji to play for Sussex as an amateur.

The club agreed to pay his hotel and out-of-pocket expenses and while there are no records of other 'payments' it is impossible to believe that someone with Ranji's immeasurable box-office appeal would not have received some sort of sinecure on top.

At the time, to play for a first-class county a player had to have been resident for two years although it was difficult to establish whether rules were being bent or not. It was up to other counties to protest and when Ranji explained that he would be moving to Eastbourne there was little reaction. But, as the following year's *Wisden* observed: "Ranji's appearance for Sussex took most people by surprise, as the fact of him qualifying for Sussex was practically unknown until the early part of May 1895."

His Sussex debut came against MCC at Lord's. After taking a catch at slip to dismiss MCC captain Grace, he scored a fluent 77 not out of a total of 219 in Sussex's first innings. Grace made a hundred in the second innings before he was caught off one of Ranji's off-breaks. He went on to take six wickets but before the close Sussex, set 405 to win, had lost a wicket and when the final day began there were fewer than 100 spectators in the ground. A Sussex defeat looked inevitable.

It was then that Sussex and English cricket at large discovered its new hero. Promoted to number four, he made 112 in the pre-lunch session and by the afternoon scored 150 of the 208 runs Sussex scored in just over two-and-a-half hours. When he was bowled by Grace he returned to the amateurs' dressing room to prolonged applause from the MCC members, whose number had grown to several hundred as news of Ranji's astonishing performance spread on the telegraph wires and in the early editions of the evening papers. He remains one of only seven Sussex batsman to score a century on their debut for the county, having previously played first-class cricket elsewhere.

MCC won the game by 19 runs but cricket had found itself a star and soon Ranji was winning admirers throughout England. That summer, as he appeared on grounds he had never played on for the first time, word of mouth ensured he would do so in front of big crowds. Even Grace, who at the age of 47 was enjoying a return to the form of his halcyon days, found his achievements completely overshadowed, despite scoring more runs (2,346 at 51) compared to Ranji's 1,775 at 49. The statistics, certainly as far as the sporting public were concerned, had become an irrelevance.

It wasn't always easy for Ranji though. Five days after the MCC match he got so cold in the field at Trent Bridge he stopped the ball with his feet when it came near him and kept his hands in his pockets. When a sudden snow storm swept over the ground his team-mates had to ply him with brandy and smother him in blankets to keep him warm by the pavilion fire.

He made 1,775 runs that summer at an average of 49.31. *Wisden* reported that "he scarcely ever looked back from his brilliant start, quickly became accustomed to the strange surroundings of county cricket and scored heavily against all classes of bowling. His wonderful placing on the leg side was quite disheartening for the leading professionals who were unaccustomed to seeing their best ball turned to the boundary for four."

On the more benign pitches of the County Ground, where the short square boundaries encouraged high scoring, Ranji soon made himself at home. Crowds of up to 10,000, most of whom had never seen a black man before – never mind one who was supposedly an Indian prince – flocked to the ground. Ranji loved Brighton. He took up residence at the Norfolk Hotel, only occasionally paying his bills, while the Royal Pavilion conjured up visions of India. He loved the town's vitality and sense of style. Eastbourne? Forget it.

He started with 150 against MCC and four half-centuries which was followed a chanceless, unbeaten 137 to save the game on a broken wicket against Oxford University. Later in the season, on a pitch badly affected by rain, he scored 100 out of a total of 171 against Nottinghamshire while against Middlesex he shared his first century stand with Fry, 117 in 70 minutes. His form did tail off towards the end of the season, as the mental and physical rigours of playing so often for the first time in his career as well as the expectancy to score runs, began to take their toll.

By the end of June 1896 he had already scored five hundreds, including an innings of 146 for MCC against a Cambridge University side whose attack was led by the formidable fast bowler Jessop and who described Ranji as "just about as perfect a specimen of batsmanship as one could desire."

By then Ranji had enjoyed one of his first encounters with the touring Australians in a country-house match at Sheffield Park which attracted crowds of 50,000 including the Prince of Wales. Ranji made scores of 79 and 42 on a difficult pitch and showed that he could cope with a sharp Australian attack led by Ernie Jones, who hit several players including Grace, but not Ranji (although he dismissed him 13 times, more than any other bowler in his career).

The country-wide clamour for him to be chosen for the first Test at Lord's on 22nd June was growing but MCC refused after much prevarication, its President Lord Harris claiming that Ranjitsinhji was not of British stock and would one day return to India. On the day the Test started a subdued Ranji was bowled by Jessop for his first duck in almost two years.

There was a public outcry about MCC's decision but Ranji's admirers didn't have to wait long. In those days the county hosting the Test match picked the England team rather than a panel of selectors and while Ranji was playing for Sussex against Kent at Hastings he received a telegram from Old Trafford asking him to play. Ranji replied that he would, provided that the Australians had no objection, which they didn't.

The crowds flocked to Old Trafford with 30,000 in attendance on the first morning but Australia, who had lost the first Test at Lord's, dominated the opening two days. Despite a steady 62 by Ranji, batting at number three and one of five amateurs in England's top seven, England followed on 181 behind. At stumps on the second day he was still there but his side was trailing by 72 runs with four wickets down.

Ranji was at his peerless best the following day. Despite being hit on the ear lobe by Jones, he progressed from 50 to his maiden Test hundred in just 45 minutes and finished with an unbeaten 154, having scored 17 of his 23 boundaries in the morning session. He had become the first batsman to score a Test hundred before lunch. Australia lost seven wickets chasing their target of 125 but for the Manchester crowd the abiding memory was that of Ranji taking the Australian attack apart. *The Guardian* was effusive in its praise. "No man living has ever seen finer batting than Ranjitsinhji showed in this match," the newspaper opined. "Grace has nothing to teach him as a batsman."

Ranji, who was suffering from asthma – a complaint which dogged him throughout his life – and then trod on a carpet nail in his hotel room, was dismissed twice cheaply in the deciding Test at the Oval and was unable to take the field on the final day, when England bowled out Australia for 44 to clinch the series.

But with the spotlight, temporarily at least, off him Ranji returned to Brighton and began enjoying himself again. Batting at number seven against Lancashire because of a finger injury, he single-handedly staved off defeat with a brilliant 165. Sussex's next opponents were champions-elect Yorkshire when Ranji produced one of the best batting performances in the county's history.

The game started on Thursday 20th August with Yorkshire making 407 and when rain intervened Sussex had responded with 23-2, Ranji batting at number three and having not got off the mark. On the Saturday morning a crowd of around 1,000 were there for the start although by the end it had grown to several thousand. In the first hour Ranji utterly dominated the Yorkshire attack. The *Sussex Daily News* correspondent wrote: "In his fine display the Prince, by superb wrist play and marvellous placing on the leg side, grand driving and crisp cutting, evoked the enthusiasm of his many admirers."

The innings had resumed at 11.35am and immediately captain Murdoch was taken at slip off George Hirst, bowling from the sea end. This was a formidable Yorkshire attack, led by Hirst and also including Stanley Jackson and Bobby Peel but Ranji showed them scant regard, bringing up his 50 in just 45 minutes.

He took ten off one over from Jackson and 14 off Peel and with Billy Newham providing valuable support at the other end they took the total past 100. With the score on 150, Hirst came back into the attack. The *Sussex Daily News* reported: "In his second over the Prince, with a trio to long-leg, secured his century to prolonged and deafening applause. He had been batting for an hour and a half."

In the next over, Ernest Smith had Ranji caught at slip for exactly 100 with the total on 155. "On returning to the pavilion he was greeted with much enthusiasm," added the *Sussex Daily News*. His innings had included 18 fours and evidence that he was batting on a different level to the rest of the Sussex team came with the dismissal of the last six wickets for just 36 runs. All out for 191, Sussex began their second innings at 2.45pm on the final afternoon in arrears by 216. Fry and Billy Marlow, one of five amateurs in the Sussex team, batted cautiously and when Fry fell for 42 Ranji returned to the wicket for the second time in the day to more warm applause.

There was an early scare when he was nearly stumped off Brown but soon he began treating a crowd which had grown to around 3,000 to sumptuous stroke-play and the Yorkshire attack with utter disdain. Hawke used eight different bowlers in Sussex's second innings and clearly it had become physically difficult for Hirst and Peel, who bowled more than 30 overs each in the day, to maintain their accuracy, although they remained economical.

By the time Marlow was out for 30 the second-wicket pair had put on 72 and although there was a brief respite when Yorkshire bowled three successive maidens Ranji was soon back in full flow. "It is not often that the Yorkshire bowlers have been treated with so little respect," reported *Wisden*. "His brilliancy and determination enabled Sussex to escape honourably from their position."

For the first time in the day Ranji found a partner prepared to match him – or at least try to match him – stroke for stroke in Horsham's Ernest Killick. They wiped off the first-innings deficit as Ranji moved into the 90s by which time an exasperated Lord Hawke had thrown the ball to David Denton, who played 11 Tests for England as a batsman but had no great pretensions as a bowler.

Ranji drove him to long on for three to take his score to 99 and then took a quick single off Hirst in the next over to reach his century in five minutes shy of two hours at the crease. "The spectators cheered again and again and the Yorkshire team joined in the deafening applause," wrote the *Daily News*.

The draw having been secured, the third-wicket pair took their stand to 127 by stumps, Ranji driving the last ball of the match for four to finish on 125 not out. "After the match a large crowd assembled in front of the pavilion shouting for 'Ranji' applauding continuously," reported the *Sussex Daily News*. "The demonstration, which was of the most hearty character, was maintained for several minutes with the occupants of the pavilion joining in until the Prince was induced to come from the dressing room and acknowledge the applause."

There are no other recorded instances of an individual player scoring two hundreds on the same day of a first-class match. As Ranji achieved this 116 years ago it makes his performance even more astonishing, although he was a remarkable cricketer.

"He was an artist with an artist's eye for the game," observed CB Fry. "Ranji's big innings pleased him in proportion as each stroke approached perfection. He tried to make every stroke he played a thing of beauty."

Ranji made a total of 58 hundreds for Sussex as his legend with the country grew. He captained the side for five years between 1899 and 1903 but only played in three completed seasons after that in 1904, 1908 and 1912, passing 1,000 runs on each occasion. By then domestic responsibilities in India were taking up much more of his time, although he didn't stop making an impression.

Arthur Gilligan, a future Sussex captain, remembers being taken to the Oval in 1908 to watch his hero, by now 35 and thickening somewhat around the waist, bat for the first time.

He recalls: "Sussex batted and after what seemed like an interminable period Ranjitsinhji came down the steps to a storm of cheers and applause. I was thrilled to the core because the Jam Sahib was my hero. I can visualise him now: that elegant stance, the glorious late cut, the superb leg-glance, that lightning control of the bowling and that wonderful eye, which seemed to indicate that he could see the ball in its flight a fraction quicker than the average English player. What nectar of cricket it all was." That day Ranji scored another double hundred.

After nearly 25 years of disputed succession, Ranji had returned to India and eventually succeeded to the Nawanagar throne in 1907. He proved to be an imaginative ruler and played an important role in Indian affairs, twice representing his country at the League of Nations.

He made a brief but misguided return to Sussex cricket in 1920 when he was persuaded to play three games despite being portly and out of breath. His real motive was to see how he might do without the use of his right eye which he had lost in a shooting accident on a Yorkshire moor in 1915. Scores of 16, 9, 13 and 1 made it clear, as *Wisden* observed, that "whatever they had seen in the rotund figure of an Indian prince at the wicket it had not been Ranji." He died of a heart attack in April 1933 at the age of 60.

Ranjitsinhji's name is never far away from the pages of the Sussex record books. He made the highest score for the county against both Essex (230 in 1902) and Surrey (234 not out also in 1902) while no batsman in the county's history has made more than his 14 double hundreds. Only CB Fry (68) and John Langridge (76) made more centuries while his 1900 aggregate of 2,824 first-class runs has only been bettered by three players: Langridge, Jim Parks senior and Fry.

He scored 1,000 runs eight times including 2,000 runs on four occasions while his partnership of 344 with Newham against Essex in 1902 is still a record for the seventh wicket in England.

Ranji has been the subject of several biographies; the best Simon Wilde's exhaustively researched and acclaimed study in 1990 which was shortlisted for the Sports Book of the Year award. In it, Wilde worked diligently to uncover much more about him than his prowess on the cricket field.

Away from cricket Ranji was by no means perfect. Until he became the Jam Sahib in 1907 he was notoriously impecunious but spent lavishly and left a string of bad debts.

And, of course, when he arrived for the first time in England in 1888 his claims to princely status were tenuous to say the least. Adopted as an heir by the Jam Sahib against the ruler's failure to father one of his own, his princedom was revoked four years later and not restored for another 25 years.

But when the Victorian Age became the Edwardian Age he was the most celebrated cricketer and arguably the most celebrated sportsman in the world, notwithstanding the pre-eminence of WG Grace.

"It was the age of simple first principles, of the stout respectability of the straight bat and good-length balls," wrote Neville Cardus. "And then suddenly this visitation of supple, dusky legerdemain happened. A man who played as no one else in England could possibly have played. The honest length ball was not met by the honest straight bat but with a flick of the wrist and charmed away to the boundary."

Above all else, though, he is still remembered as one of cricket's first superstars and for a feat that is unlikely ever to be repeated in the history of the game.

CHRIS ADAMS

2007: The Longest Wait

NO OTHER TEAM competition in British sport is harder to win than the County Championship. You don't fluke it. The course lasts for five months and 16 four-day games and external factors such as the weather and international commitments can have a huge influence on the outcome.

Such is its gruelling nature, the protagonists invariably end up physically and mentally drained long before the last ball is bowled, the modest trophy held aloft by the winning captain and the equally modest cheque (the 2011 winners Lancashire won £550,000 – a top Premier League footballer's monthly salary) is banked by the treasurer.

Chris Adams remembers sleepless nights throughout the closing stages of the 2003 season, when he eventually led Sussex to the first Championship in their history. When the county played their main rivals Lancashire in the penultimate game of that season he reckons he slept for about five hours in total during six nights in his Manchester hotel room. "It was an awful time, I seriously thought about giving up the captaincy when we finally won it because the pressure had been so great," he remembers.

Four years later Adams was in his tenth season in charge and considered himself suitably battle-hardened. In the intervening years he had led Sussex to another Championship in 2006 that was only secured in the last game. It was also the year they also won their first Lord's final for 20 years after another nerve-shredder against Lancashire. He was used to winning and, he felt, accustomed to the pressures of delivering trophies to Sussex supporters who now expected success after decades of hoping for it.

"When we won it for the first time in 2003 we realised that backing it up the following year, going through all the mental agonies as well as the physical pain again a year later, was going to be extremely tough and we fell short even though we had a very good side and should probably have won the title again," remembers Adams.

"Winning the Championship is hard graft. I don't think winning any other major sports title in this country is more difficult. People in other sports don't realise just how draining it can be. Of course there are periods in any game when you are not directly involved but for a captain there is always something that needs doing."

Adams may have been celebrating a decade as captain in 2007 but it almost felt as if he had to prove himself all over again – to his players, the management at Hove and those expectant supporters.

The celebrations which marked their 2006 Championship win had barely died down when Yorkshire officials courted Adams, appropriately enough on the dance floor of the Royal Albert Hall during the Professional Cricketers' Association end-of-season presentation dinner. One of the traditional powerhouses of the English game, Yorkshire were fed up that smaller, less well-resourced counties such as Sussex were winning trophies their expectant membership seemed still to regard was their birthright.

Coach David Byas, who had taken his no-nonsense reputation as a player into coaching, recognised in Adams a kindred spirit and told his bosses to try and lure him to Headingley, although Chief Executive Stewart Regan expected to be given short shrift when he made his move. Adams was the most successful captain in Sussex's history and feted throughout the county. His family was settled and he hoped one day when his playing career was over to take up a coaching or management role at Hove.

The conversation barely lasted a minute but Adams gave Regan his number and a few days later they met in London with Yorkshire Chairman Colin Graves. The offer was financially lucrative and, more importantly, gave Adams carte blanche to run the cricket at one of the biggest clubs in the country as captain and Director of Cricket.

Or so he thought. Adams accepted the offer and in early October told a stunned Sussex he would be leaving six weeks after he had led the county to the double.

"I remember talking to the then Chairman David Green who told me 'All that glistens is not necessarily gold'. I still recall those words because he turned out to be spot on. I don't think he was referring to the financial offer which might have been luring me away. It was more about what was being promised to me on the cricket side. I was going to have a serious power base, especially at a county like Yorkshire."

A press conference was called to confirm the appointment but when he sat down to face the media Adams was already having serious doubts. Having asked at earlier meetings with his new employers that they bring back Darren Lehmann and fellow Australian Jason Gillespie he was stunned to learn in a two-minute conversation with Graves just before facing the cameras that the Chairman had instead signed Younis Khan as overseas player without consulting him.

Adams recalls: "It was too late to pull out of the press conference but I just knew there would be too many battles to be fought and this was a situation where the Chief Executive and Chairman were doing what they wanted and that I had been signed to placate the Yorkshire members and to keep people happy. People who saw the press conference told me afterwards that my expression suggested something wasn't right."

Now it was Yorkshire's turn to be surprised as Adams confirmed his about-turn. Fortunately, he had not signed a contract and Sussex welcomed him back with open arms. Coach Mark Robinson described it as the best news he'd had for ages. "It was the hardest decision I have ever had to make in my career," said Adams. I just didn't feel as committed and inspired about pulling on another county's shirt as I should have done. They say never let your heart rule your head but throughout all of that my heart completely turned my head around."

It was a humbling experience nonetheless for Adams, having to effectively ask Sussex for his old job back, and when the players gathered again for the start of 2007 season he had to galvanise a squad who, a few weeks earlier, thought they were going to be led by a different captain.

"It took me down a peg or two," says Adams. "I thought I might have lost a bit of respect with the players but, to their credit, when we met up again I think they understood the situation and the reasons why I reversed my decision. I sat down and was very honest with them. But you still have to look them in the eye and say 'We know what it takes to win the Championship – can we do it again with me in charge?'

"We knew that still equated to six months of working your nuts off, especially the first three months, and making a lot of sacrifices. We would have to stay tight as a unit and work hard for each other. We knew that we still perhaps lacked high-end ability but we made up for that in commitment and finding the way to win a game."

Perhaps the biggest change for Adams was the way it affected his relationship with Robinson, who had succeeded Peter Moores in 2006.

"I'd been in the job for a long time and by then I did a lot of things without thinking about them because they didn't take much out of me mentally or physically," Adams says.

"Things like what pitch were we going to use, the condition of the nets, team selection, what time we did warm-ups, what we'd do if we won the toss - a lot of that I was doing on automatic pilot.

"At that stage of his coaching career Mark wanted more responsibility and I was happy to let him have it so he started to consult the groundsman about the wicket. Peter Moores was very clear about what team he wanted and I would have to work hard to try and influence his thinking if I wanted to change it.

"With Robbo it was completely different. For instance, he would often lean on me to make the final call about the side. Back then he realised how important the senior players were to our team so rather than coach and captain he would bring

Mushy, Yardy and Goodwin into the mix when we discussed selection and other issues. It was different and I was happy about it. I had got past the stage where it was me leading and everyone following – it was now the time for me to encourage others to lead.

"It is why 2007 was one of my best years as captain. I was still able to exert an influence on the others and impart my authority when it needed to be done but I could also delegate and know that it wouldn't have a detrimental effect on the way we did things as a team."

Sussex's first two titles had been achieved without too many of those external distractions intervening. The England selectors by and large left the squad alone, they only used 15 players – four of whom played in less than half of their 16 games in 2003 – and it was one of the hottest and driest summers for years. In 2006 17 players were used.

But 2007 was different. Four members of the squad played for England. Matt Prior made his Test debut (with a hundred at Lord's), Luke Wright and Mike Yardy were regulars in the one-day squad and James Kirtley earned a surprise recall in England's 'horses for courses' selection for the inaugural Twenty20 World Cup in South Africa.

For the title decider against Worcestershire in September they were down to their last 13 available players as injuries took their toll. Goodwin, Rana Naved and Saqlain Mushtaq were all sidelined, forcing Sussex to give a Championship debut to left-arm seam bowler Chris Liddle.

The weather proved problematic too. Sussex lost the equivalent of ten full days including all four against Surrey in late August. Adams was phlegmatic as he watched the rain pour down at the Oval: "Until someone comes up with a way of making it not rain between April and September on cricket grounds you have to put up with it – and we did."

And even before a ball was bowled Adams had to deal with a personal crisis crowding in on his most important player, Mushtaq Ahmed.

In March Mushtaq was with the Pakistan squad for the World Cup in the West Indies. Hours after they had lost to Ireland – a result which effectively knocked them out of the tournament – coach Bob Woolmer, who had brought in Mushtaq as part of his backroom team, was found dead in his hotel room in Kingston, Jamaica. It was another three months before an investigation decided that Woolmer had died of natural causes. In the meantime all manner of fanciful theories were put forward for the cause of death, including a bizarre claim that he had been poisoned by champagne from two bottles given to him by Mushtaq.

Amazingly, Mushtaq was back at Hove a few weeks later and took ten wickets as Sussex began the season with a win over Kent. But he claimed just six in his next three games and when he briefly returned to Lahore to try and escape the speculation by spending time with his family he was besieged by journalists investigating the latest crackpot theories into Woolmer's death. Only in June, when official confirmation came through, could Mushtaq put the episode behind him but he had thought seriously about retirement.

"It was a very hard few weeks for Mushy, but when he went on the pitch that was his escape in many ways," says Adams. "He'd played such a massive part with 101 wickets in 2006 but even after all the Woolmer business died down he wasn't quite the same. You could almost see it in his eyes – he knew he would have to bowl all those overs again and he wasn't quite as fit as he'd been. But he was willing to make the sacrifice. Mushy always responded to me and the fact he ended up with 90 wickets that season despite all those distractions speaks volumes for the man."

Yardy broke his finger in the annual curtain-raiser against MCC at Lord's while Lewry was recovering from a virus which left him a stone lighter. Sussex beat Kent by eight wickets in their first game but it was a false dawn. For the first time in a decade they followed it with back-to-back Championship defeats, both by an innings, against Warwickshire and Kent. When Surrey made 626-3, the highest total at Hove since 2002, in their next game another damaging defeat loomed but Murray Goodwin batted through the final day for an unbeaten 205 and Sussex saved the game. It was a pivotal moment in the season.

Two wins – one against Hampshire against Arundel when a rejuvenated Mushtaq took nine wickets – and two draws left Sussex second at the three-week Twenty20 hiatus and when four-day action resumed at Horsham in early July Sussex thrashed Durham by an innings and 102 runs in three days to stay second, a point behind Yorkshire.

The gap had increased to 16 points after Sussex drew a badly rain-affected game at the Rose Bowl. Bad weather around the country meant Sussex's Horsham triumph had been the only positive result since the resumption of the Championship but in their next game Adams played a key role in a victory which suffused them with the belief that they could win the title again.

On their previous visit to the well-appointed Aigburth ground in South Liverpool, Lancashire had beaten Sussex inside two days and fancied their chances of doing it again and taking control of the Championship race. While Sussex had to leave out Luke Wright, who had torn his groin on the wet outfield at the Rose Bowl, Lancashire fielded eight internationals including Andrew Flintoff and Muttiah Muralitharan.

"It was the game which defined the season and the one when I knew we would have a chance of winning the Championship again," says Adams. "It was one of the greatest matches I have played in because of the sheer quality of some of the one-on-one battles that took place over those three days.

"How Lancashire didn't win the title with that side is unbelievable. When you compare that team to the one which did win it in 2011 it's amazing really, I suppose it says a lot for Peter Moores' coaching skills."

The defining moment in the defining match came shortly after tea on the third day when Adams took what he considered to be the best – and certainly most important – of the 404 catches he took in his first-class career. Flintoff and Stuart Law – so often Sussex's nemesis in the past – were taking their side towards a victory target of 242 when Adams held a stunning catch, one-handed to his left inches from the turf to dismiss Law off the bowling of Rana Naved. Lancashire folded and Sussex won by 108 runs.

"I wasn't surprised to take it but the reaction catches are always magical moments," says Adams. "You don't have time to think about them and when they stick it is wonderful. All slip catches are difficult – it is a question of the degree of hardness. All I did was dive to my left and throw my hand out at full tilt. It stuck a couple of inches above the ground and we had got their best player out.

"It's funny, because I also remember that game for something as much as the catch. When they batted again I brought Mushy on after three overs which they totally were not expecting. He got four wickets in their second innings and after we got Law out it was a fairly straightforward victory. I knew we could win the title after that game. It was played with such intensity and almost like a Test match at times."

Sussex returned to the top of the table but they were soon disabused of any notion that there would be a smooth run-in to the title. Richard Montgomerie's 195 on the final day staved off defeat to Warwickshire at Hove and they then spent four frustrating days watching the rain fall at the Oval. Meanwhile, Yorkshire were thrashing Warwickshire to open up a 14-point lead ahead of the meeting of third versus first at Hove in early September.

Like their roses rivals a month earlier, Yorkshire fielded a top-heavy team including Inzamam-ul-Haq, Michael Vaughan, Matthew Hoggard, Jacques Rudolph and Imran Tahir but they were ground into submission on the first two days by hundreds from Yardy and Andrew Hodd and then by Mushtaq Ahmed and Saqlain Mushtaq. Dismissed for 247 and 89, they had lost by an innings by 3.30pm on the third day.

Sussex headed to the Riverside for their penultimate game protecting a five-point lead at a ground where they had never lost before and initially things went well. Put in, they reached 115-2 but lost eight wickets in the afternoon on the first day during some frenetic batting.

Five overs into the afternoon session on the second day Rana Naved hurtled around the boundary and in trying to make a diving stop badly dislocated his shoulder. Play was held up for 35 minutes and an ambulance made its way to treat the stricken bowler across the outfield. At first, Adams thought it might be a career-ending rather than just a season-ending injury for his main fast bowler.

"It wasn't pleasant to see an ambulance on the pitch," says Adams. "He was in a lot of pain but also shock, every time he moved his shoulder he was in agony. Everyone thought his career was over, never mind his season. It was his bowling arm and when you did the damage that he did you're going to struggle to come back from it. To recover as he did and play again five months later showed a lot about his character."

Rana was fit enough to return to Sussex with his team-mates, wincing in agony every time the coach went over a bump, but he wasn't the only casualty. By now Lewry was playing with the help of five painkillers a day because of knee problems, Adams had a badly bruised hand and both Mushtaq and Saqlain Mushtaq were hobbling because of groin and knee injuries.

A nine-wicket defeat also meant Sussex had lost their lead going into the final game. Lancashire led them by six points with Durham a further 2.5 points behind. The Championship was between those three and Adams almost felt a sense of relief as Sussex headed back down the A1.

"It was a struggle going into the last game," he recalls. "We lost but we didn't think the title had gone. In fact it simplified things – we knew we had to beat Worcestershire and rely on other results. Lancashire were in a great position but even then they always allowed themselves to be distracted by things they could not control such as the weather, which they were always moaning about. But with us finishing at Hove and them at the Oval they couldn't even use that as an excuse when the last round of games started."

On 19th September the last round of fixtures started with five counties still in with a chance of silverware, although Hampshire and Yorkshire were relying on various other results going their way.

Adams was always going to play despite his hand injury but Saqlain was ruled out and Sussex were dealt another blow when Goodwin had to fly to Perth because of a family bereavement. The man who hit the winning runs in 2003 would be 8,000 miles away for the denouement four years later.

An already-relegated Worcestershire side was expected to prove compliant opposition even against an under-strength team and on an overcast first day Richard Montgomerie joined Goodwin and Adams in passing 1,000 runs for the season. For Adams, the milestone was more relevant than it had been on the eight previous occasions he had reached it.

He says: "Remember, the most important part of a captain's job is to be able to deliver his skill to the highest possible standard and because we were a bit more democratic as a squad in terms of decision-making I was able to maintain my own standards with the bat. The last five years of my career from a batting perspective were not stellar years but they were good years. I found a way of getting runs."

Sussex closed the first day on a strong position on 287-4 while up at the Oval Mark Ramprakash, so often a thorn in their side, was unbeaten on 180 for Surrey against Lancashire having been dropped without scoring. The next morning Sussex added a further 164 in 27 overs as the tail gave Robin Martin-Jenkins valuable support. To the horror of a sizeable crowd, including his father reporting on his last game for *The Times* before retirement, Martin-Jenkins was last out for 99 but Sussex still totalled 532. Worcestershire needed 383 just to avoid the follow-on with the pitch dry and crusty but they got through to stumps on 96-2, 20 overs having been lost to bad light.

On the third day Mushtaq got to work. A googly did for Graeme Hick, in what was his last appearance at Hove, and the last five wickets went down in 9.4 overs. Mushtaq finished with 6-93 and Worcestershire were all out for 213 and would follow on 319 behind. The only thing that could deny Sussex now was the weather.

Or so it seemed. Adams sensed complacency and rallied his troops. "I remember having to deliver reasonably strong words during that third day because it was going well and I felt we'd accepted that we would win as a matter of course," he says. "They were already relegated and trying one or two youngsters out but all our focus seemed to be on what was happening at the Oval. We had to get serious and we worked hard to get the result."

While Ramprakash was batting Surrey into a seemingly impregnable position with another century in their second innings, Sussex worked their way through Worcestershire's resistance. Worcestershire ended the third day on 190-5 but there was mild surprise in the Sussex dressing room when they came off to hear that Surrey had declared before the close and set Lancashire 493 to win and they made 27 of them without loss from ten overs.

The end, for Worcestershire at least, came at 12.23pm on the final day – a warm, sunny Saturday. Mushtaq finished with 7-132 and 13 wickets in the match. With 90 victims, he was the leading wicket-taker in the Championship for the fifth year in a row and his early-season travails were well behind him.

Now all Sussex could do was wait. As the players left the field it was announced that Montgomerie had played his final game and would be retiring to take up a teaching job at Eton College.

He led the players on to the balcony to take the applause when another announcement was made. Sussex would be presented with the trophy at 5.15pm if they were champions. It was going to be a long afternoon.

"It was hard to know what to do that afternoon," remembers Adams. "I had no desire to go anywhere. There was no more cricket so it was time to have a few beers as a squad and with the sponsors and families. A lot of people were hanging around outside though which I found a little surprising." Martin-Jenkins took refuge in the Jacuzzi and four Lancashire wickets fell. "The hot-tub was bringing me luck but I was getting eaten alive by the chlorine," he remembers.

Around 1,000 Sussex supporters settled in for the vigil. With no Sky pictures available in the ground because the coverage had switched to an interactive channel the only way to monitor the scores was through occasional radio updates (this being a Saturday afternoon the focus was almost entirely on football), rely on phonecalls to friends who did have the option of using the red button at home or the main scoreboard at Hove which was doing its best to replicate events at the Oval.

An impromptu game of cricket involving several players and some youngsters began on the outfield but concentration on anything else but events 55 miles north was difficult. At 2.45pm, Lancashire had made 271-3 thanks mainly to a hundred by VVS Laxman. An inexperienced Surrey attack was being dismantled but just before tea Law and Steven

Croft fell in successive overs. At the break, Lancashire were 308-5.

Back at Hove, every Surrey success was greeted by a vociferous roar. Glen Chapple was sixth out, leaving Lancashire needing 131 to win, and the new ball accounted for Luke Sutton. When the statutory last hour started Lancashire needed 69 from 15 overs then 58 from 12 but they lost two more wickets. Dominic Cork was left with last man Gary Keedy with 37 required from 12 overs.

As the cheers got louder so the tension increased. "By now it had become a vigil in the dressing room for the players and a few of the lads were getting nicely oiled," remembered Adams. "As Lancashire wickets started to tumble the roars got stronger. Brighton were playing Yeovil that day and a lot of the fans came back after the game and the atmosphere was a bit like a football match by then.

"I remember Robbo coming in when they got eight or nine down and weren't that far away. It was pure agony and as a coach now I know what that must have felt like for him. As players you do your bit on the field whereas for a coach it seems to matter that much more because they aren't in control. He was pacing around like an expectant father outside the delivery room.

"Every time a wicket went down we hoped it was Dominic Cork because he was a proper competitor and while he was in there was always that feeling that Lancashire might do it. When someone rushed in and said 'Corky's out!' I thought 'This is it' but unfortunately it was Luke Sutton."

By now the most effective method of monitoring events at the Oval was the scoreboard at Hove which ticked over with every run and wicket. One more roar... please.

Finally, at 6.02pm and five hours and 39 minutes after Mushtaq had wrapped up victory over Worcestershire, Cork played on and Surrey had won by 24 runs.

At Hove there was bedlam. Adams recalls: "I was sitting in my seat in the dressing room when Robbo, who had been on the phone to his parents, came bursting in. 'Cork's out! I remember Mike Yardy jumping on me followed by Jason Lewry. It was a big release."

Sussex had won their third Championship with a modest seven victories over the season but no one was worrying about that when Adams and his players emerged onto the balcony in front of a crowd that had grown to around 1,500 and started spraying champagne around.

The car with the trophy, which had been stationed at Gatwick Airport ready to head north or south, made its way to Hove and shortly before 7pm and in fading light Adams lifted it and showed it to an exultant crowd for the third time in his career.

A year earlier Sussex had sealed their second Championship on a damp Friday lunchtime in Nottingham. The party went on for the rest of the day but there is nothing like winning a trophy on your own turf, especially when there is a convenient party venue right on your doorstep.

By 8pm the Sussex Cricketer pub at the entrance to the ground was heaving. As the players, committee members and backroom staff made their way in they were greeted like warriors returning victorious from the battlefield. The trophy itself was filled and re-filled with champagne and passed around the bar like a loving cup.

The following day came the now-familiar open-top bus ride around the streets of Brighton and Hove. "That was tough," laughs Adams. "We were all wearing dark glasses and very much the worse for wear. I was always worried when we did the parade whether anyone would turn up but that was probably the most enjoyable of the three we had. It was a Sunday afternoon, the weather was good and there were lots of people out and about and they all seemed to know what we had achieved which was very gratifying."

A year later it was all over for Adams, fittingly enough after he had led Sussex to their eighth trophy in 11 seasons in charge. He handed over the captaincy to Mike Yardy and a few weeks later was heading into his first management role not, as he had hoped, at Hove but at the Oval as Surrey's Director of Cricket.

"What we achieved together at Sussex is something I will never forget," he reflects now, three years after leaving the county. "Nothing will ever top winning the Championship for the first time but winning it for the third time in 2007 took a lot of courage by the players. We had a lot of setbacks that season and it took me a while to get back to how I wanted to do things as captain after what had gone on with Yorkshire during the winter.

"Was it a triumph against the odds? Definitely. It was probably a watershed for that Sussex side as well. Monty retired and Mushy followed next year but it was a wonderful achievement because until that final Lancashire wicket fell on the last day of the season we were always up against it to a certain extent."

The Championship has come up with a couple more last-day thrillers since then without quite capturing the drama played out on that September afternoon at the Oval and Hove. "Sussex supporters always remembered where they were when

Murray Goodwin hit the four to win the title in 2003 and I suspect it was the same for 2007," said Adams. "Winning it for the third time fulfilled me as a captain. It was easily the hardest to win but when we did it tasted even sweeter. We'd been through the mill a bit as a squad that year and to finish up with another trophy, and in such circumstances, will be something everyone involved will never forget."

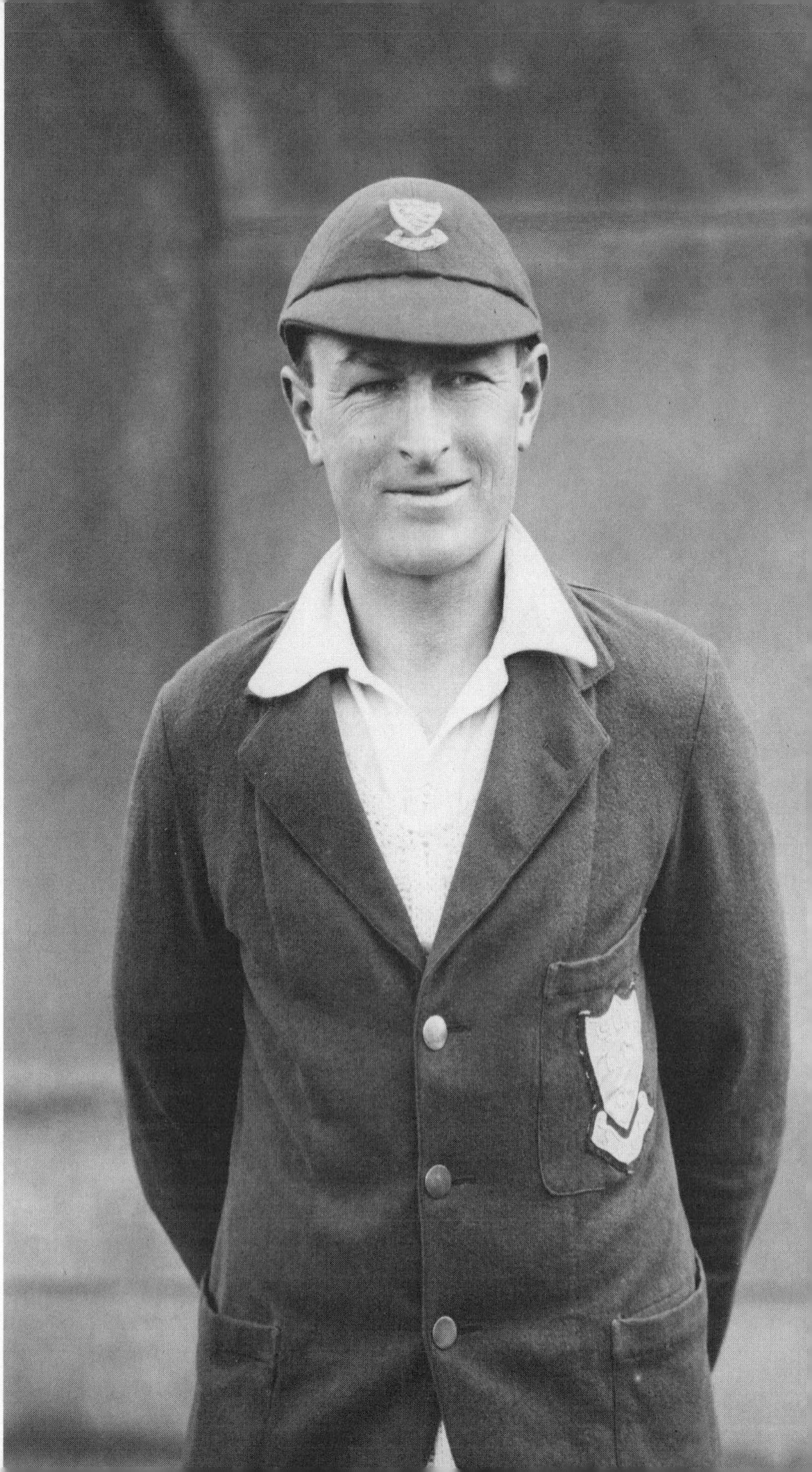

JIM PARKS SNR

1939: The Show Must Go On

IT SHOULD HAVE been the perfect end to the summer. The champion county, Yorkshire, was in town for Brighton & Hove Cricket Week and Sussex supporters were paying tribute to one of the county's finest servants, Jim Parks senior, who had chosen it as his benefit match.

Jim's son, "Young Jim" – he was seven at the time – remembers being taken to the County Ground to watch Dad in action on the second day of the game, a Thursday.

"The ground was pretty full even though it was a working day," he recalled. "I remember being at the top end in glorious sunshine watching this great Yorkshire side with Len Hutton, Bill Bowes and Hedley Verity – all names I had read about or Dad had talked about – and thinking it was the most marvellous thing." The next afternoon Verity took seven wickets for just nine runs in 48 balls as Sussex were bowled out for 33. Verity, arguably the finest left-arm spinner English cricket has ever produced, would finish the last season of the 1930s as he had the first – his debut summer in county cricket – as the leading wicket-taker with 191 victims.

At such an impressionable age Jim was already in love with the game but the reminders of a greater peril had never been far away in that summer of 1939. The senior basement playroom at his school, St Wilfrids in Haywards Heath, had been turned into an air-raid shelter and the pupils issued with gas masks.

* * * * *

It says a lot about the players involved that the last game of cricket in England before the outbreak of the Second World War was as competitive and hard-fought as it was, at least until the final afternoon when Verity wreaked havoc on a drying pitch.

A terrifying conflict was imminent – everyone seemed to appreciate that – so for the players and spectators it seemed more important than usual to have some vestige of normal life to enjoy before the onset of war. The distinguished journalist RC Robertson-Glasgow wrote: "Cricket followers turned as to an old friend who gives you a seat, a glass of beer and something sane to think about."

The *Sussex Daily News* page lead on Saturday 2nd September, the day before war broke out, began with the word "Lamentable". It was not a comment on the Sussex batting in the face of Verity's brilliance or even Prime Minister Neville Chamberlain's efforts at appeasement with Hitler. Rather, the word was used by the county's Chairman GS Godfree to describe the response to an appeal for funds in the club's centenary year. Sussex had distributed 15,000 fundraising 'Centenary Cards' and only 350 had been returned.

"Something has got to be done about it," remarked Godfree at the club's annual dinner which still went ahead on that Friday evening at the Old Ship Hotel in Brighton. "Some of us are getting rather tired," he added. "If the people of Sussex do not want first-class cricket we will throw up our hands and they won't get first-class cricket."

Alongside it on the broadsheet page was a nine-paragraph report simply headed "Sussex All Out for 33".

The dinner was attended by most of the Sussex players humbled earlier that day by Verity, including beneficiary Jim Parks. He might have nodded sagely when his chairman made his remarks about the apparent lack of financial support for cricket in the county. In those days there were no benefit dinners or golf days, no auctions or wine-tasting trips which are the mainstays of the modern beneficiary's calendar. Instead, pre-war beneficiaries (and for years to come after it) would raise money paying visits to pubs and local cricket clubs and rely mostly on the generosity of working men. "And in those days there wasn't a lot of spare cash about," recalled Young Jim. "If you came home from an evening doing a quiz or a talk at a pub with a few quid you'd had a decent night."

The main fundraiser back then was the beneficiary's match and in that regard Jim Parks had chosen wisely. Yorkshire were the team of the 1930s, having won the County Championship seven times. Only twice did the trophy leave Headingley during the decade – Lancashire won it in 1934 (a triumph that would take them 77 years to repeat outright) and Derbyshire were the champions two years later. Yorkshire's 1939 title completed a hat-trick of wins.

It was the last game of the season and, as former captain Hugh Bartlett remembered: "The bands played on the outfield, the marquees were decorated and teas taken." A collection for Jim on the final day raised £75 taking his total benefit to a princely £734. Today, that would be the equivalent of £36,000 – a sum most modern-day beneficiaries, even humble country pros, would hope to raise in a couple of events. At least Jim had the foresight to insure the match against bad weather for £250.

These days, the distraction of running a benefit is often given as a reason why players underperform on the pitch. A convenient excuse perhaps, but there could be little other reason to explain why the summer of 1939 was one of Jim Parks' poorest in a career which brought him more than 21,000 first-class runs including 41 centuries.

He had done the double of 1,000 runs and 100 wickets for the first time four years earlier and in 1937 he threw himself into his cricket after his wife Irene had died of tuberculosis in October 1936. That summer he scored 3,003 runs and took 101 wickets with his off-cutters and in-swingers. His form earned him an England cap when he opened with a young Len Hutton at Lord's against New Zealand.

A mainstay of the Sussex side for more than a decade, Jim turned 36 a few weeks after the 1939 season began. Perhaps age was beginning to take its toll. In 1938 Jim still scored 1,740 runs at 37.82 including four hundreds but his benefit season brought him 1,108 runs – his lowest aggregate since 1932. He averaged a modest 24.08 with only one hundred, although he still played in 31 first-class games and his place in the side was never in doubt because he could still contribute with the ball. That season he took 83 wickets, his third-highest return in a career now into its 16th season.

Any hopes that Sussex might celebrate their 100th anniversary with a tilt at Yorkshire's supremacy didn't last long. They won ten games that year, including four in August, and finished tenth but the best days of a side which had finished runners-up three times earlier in the decade were clearly receding.

Jim's best performance of the year had come with the ball when he took 5-27 against Gloucestershire at Bristol. His only hundred was against Worcestershire at Eastbourne nine days before his benefit game when he made 115 not out in an eight-wicket win. "I was there for that game," remembers his son. "John Langridge hit out on the last afternoon and Hugh Bartlett won us the game in the final hour."

In contrast to Sussex's stuttering form, Yorkshire had swept all before them. Hove was the last stop on a southern tour that had begun at Dover where Verity took nine wickets as Yorkshire won after being put in.

"At Dover the outbreak of war seemed imminent every minute," wrote the doyen of Yorkshire cricket chroniclers, Jim Kilburn. "Boys came to the ground with telegraphs almost in procession with orders for reservists to report for duty. Cricket was a secondary topic among players and spectators."

Yorkshire then travelled to Bournemouth where they twice bowled out Hampshire for 116. Verity took 6-22 in the first innings and Yorkshire, who had made a modest 243, still won by an innings.

By now the country knew war was inevitable. Yorkshire batsman Herbert Sutcliffe, a reserve officer, headed back to Yorkshire instead of along the south coast for the season's finale after being called up.

Skipper Brian Sellers called his squad together and they decided to play the game at Hove, not least because they didn't want to let down Jim Parks. "We are entertainers and until we have had instructions to the contrary we will carry on," he insisted.

It wasn't a sentiment shared by the rest of the cricketing world. With seven games of their tour still to play, the West Indies sailed for home. Other county games were called off and the Scarborough Festival was cancelled.

As German forces massed on the Polish border, Sussex versus Yorkshire began as scheduled at 11.30am on Wednesday 30th August 1939, and a crowd of 4,000 turned up for the first day in glorious sunshine.

In *The Times*, Dudley Carew wrote: "Hove was crowded, but nothing like as crowded had there been no threat to Poland. Groups of people gathered around cars parked in the ground listening to the wireless as it spoke of the hopeless, last-minute efforts to save a peace that was beyond aid."

Jim Kilburn was another scribe trying to concentrate on the matter in hand. "The weather behaved itself most admirably for the opening of the benefit match for James Parks," he wrote in the *Yorkshire Post*. "A considerable number of guests (paying guests of course) broiled upon the benches, sheltered in the stands or lay scattered on the grass to watch cricket of unfailing interest. Cricket for cricket's own sweet sake, with Championship cares dead and buried."

Jack Holmes won the toss and Sussex made 387, the highest score against Yorkshire that season. In keeping with a disappointing summer with the bat, Jim Parks made just two coming in at number six but Sussex were sustained by a brilliant innings from George Cox junior with even Verity struggling to tame him.

He came in with Sussex 89-2 after Cox had added 69 with John Langridge before Langridge was run out for 60 when Cox drove Verity to mid-off, set off for a single and turned to see his partner run out by Wilf Barber's direct hit. "In the afternoon Cox expressed his apologies clearly and handsomely," wrote Kilburn.

James Langridge and Parks both fell cheaply but Cox and Hugh Bartlett added 61 for the sixth wicket. Cox was well into his stride now, hammering the bowling to all parts. He scored 28 in ten minutes after lunch to reach his half-century and his hundred, which he reached just before Bartlett was bowled for 24, came in two hours and ten minutes.

Even Verity was harshly treated. Cox, demonstrating the muscular hitting his father had occasionally employed in Sussex's lower order, smashed him high over long on for six. That year the Championship experimented with eight-ball overs and in 18 of them Verity conceded 108 runs, only picking up the wickets of Holmes and Billy Griffith towards the end. The innings was not all about brutal power. "Elegant cuts and some extremely fine-placed shots just wide of third man helped provide him with a total of 198," reported the *Sussex Daily News*.

Dudley Carew was equally impressed in *The Times*. He wrote: "Concentration on the cricket was fitful yet Cox's strokes through the covers insisted on drawing attention to themselves. They were played in the grand manner and again and again the ball came rattling up against the pavilion rails."

The sagacious Kilburn, not used perhaps to seeing his beloved Yorkshire put to the sword, was a little more guarded in his praise. He wrote: "At times Cox knew fortune, but then his method invited the co-operation of fortune. When he could not reasonably drive he was prepared to cut and if the slips once or twice stretched up expectant hands, many of the boundaries gathered were as faultless as they were beautiful."

The sight of Cox in full flow was to become a familiar one for Kilburn and the Yorkshire team for young George loved batting against the White Rose, the challenge of facing the best county attack of his generation seeming to bring the best out of him. In 1938 Bartlett had taken 157 off the Australians that included a 57-minute hundred that put him in contention for the Walter Lawrence Trophy, awarded for the fastest century of the season. The next game was against Yorkshire when Bartlett, who was not playing, was presented with a gold cup for the quickest fifty of the summer before the start of play.

Cox took up the challenge of outscoring Bartlett, encouraged it seems by Sutcliffe, Yorkshire's prolific opening batsman. Having watched the ceremony, Sutcliffe remarked to Sussex secretary Lance Knowles: "It's not the end of the season yet, there is young George remember."

With Langridge occupying the sheet anchor role, as he had done for Bartlett against the Australians, Cox went on the offensive against an attack including Verity and Bill Bowes. His 50 came in 28 minutes and 25 minutes later he had moved onto 95 with some savage hitting. Six runs in three minutes and the Lawrence Trophy would be his. Maurice Leyland came on and bowled a rank long hop. "I could have hit it anywhere," remembered Cox. Instead, he mis-hit out into the deep and Wilf Barber ran around the boundary to restrict him to a single. Langridge got out and skipper Holmes, urged by the crowd to get a move on as he made his way to the wicket, came in but time had beaten Cox. He duly got to three figures, but that missed six and the fall of Langridge's wicket had taken up too much time. His hundred took three minutes more than Bartlett's.

Of his 50 hundreds for Sussex, six came against Yorkshire including 212 and 121 (both not out) in 1949, 143 in 1950 and 144 in 1953. Cox rated that 1938 performance as his finest innings for Sussex, better than his 198 a year later when a Hove crowd desperate for a pleasant distraction lapped up the entertainment.

"War was upon us," said Jim Parks, "And it was no longer possible to ignore the war bulletins. The guns had started in Poland and the tension was awful. There was a feeling we shouldn't be playing cricket but there was a festival atmosphere. We knew that this was to be our last taste of freedom for many years so we enjoyed ourselves while we could."

The Sussex faithful dug deep when the tins were rattled as a collection for the beneficiary at tea raised £75. "Please give them a big thank-you," Parks told the man from the *Sussex Daily News*. "Not only was I surprised at the size of the crowd but also for the magnificent support for the collection on my behalf."

The celebratory mood continued. A few moments after Sussex had been dismissed for 387 it was announced that Cox was to marry his sweetheart Eve Ansell in the family church at Warnham the following month, to warm applause from the spectators. "Had Jim Parks been a magician he could not have staged his benefit match to better purpose," said the *Sussex Daily News*. "Brilliant weather, a wonderful 198 from Cox and a big crowd were a joint tribute to a fine cricketer." Of Sussex's last 121 runs, Cox contributed 90 of them. He was ninth out when he square cut the off-spin of Ellis Robinson to the gully, the innings ending off the next delivery.

Before the close, Yorkshire had reached 112-1 in reply in 75 minutes. Ominously for Sussex, Len Hutton was unbeaten on 55.

In the early hours of Thursday morning the good weather broke and Hove was hit by heavy rain. With only the wicket-ends covered the pitch took a good soaking. There was no chance of an immediate resumption on the second day yet a crowd of 2,000 still turned up and Parks' benefit coffers were enhanced by a collection which raised another £26.

The war news remained grim. Holed up in their hotel while they waited for a break in the weather, the Yorkshire players fretted. "All through the morning in our hotel we were anxiously discussing the cables from Poland and Germany, which made it plain a world war was just about to begin," said Norman Yardley. "We managed to restart the game but it was played with many men's minds elsewhere. But to Yorkshiremen cricket is cricket and when we get out on the field our job is to win the game, no matter whether the heavens are falling."

The heavens having opened and done their worst, play resumed at 3.30pm and Hutton and his partner Arthur Mitchell had little difficulty against a modest Sussex attack, although Mitchell's 14 runs in the first 50 minutes suggests batting initially was not easy, particularly against Jim Langridge's under-rated left-arm spin and Parks himself.

"Conditions were entirely altered," wrote Kilburn. "Whereas on day one the ball had come through comfortably and according to reason now it moved sluggishly from the pitch and at varying and illogical heights."

Hutton, one of the finest players on drying surfaces, soon worked out what to do. Yardley recalled: "Len came down the wicket to Langridge, drove and pulled, square-cut and late-cut when he changed his length, and we were edified by the sight of a great bowler on a heaven-sent wicket being slammed all over the place."

While Mitchell settled for quiet accumulation Hutton was soon racing towards his 12th century of the summer. In two hours 15 minutes Hutton made 103 with 14 boundaries and it was a surprise, not least to the bowler himself, when he missed an attempted sweep and was trapped leg before by Cox, the fifth bowler used by Sussex. Mitchell, Maurice Leyland and Yardley all made half-centuries either side of tea and when stumps were drawn shortly after 7pm Yorkshire's reply had reached 330-3, 57 runs behind with a day to go.

A couple of Friday's newspapers made optimistic claims that war could still be avoided but the people sensed otherwise. Early in the day Lancashire's match against Surrey at Old Trafford was abandoned and matches due to start that morning were also called off. The Yorkshire committee sent a telegram to captain Sellers suggesting they pull out and head home early. Sellers' response was, once again, that as it was Parks' benefit they would prefer to continue. His club reluctantly agreed.

Under a blazing sun Yorkshire's first innings folded alarmingly. As a portent for what was to come, Langridge recovered from his second-day mauling to take four wickets. Parks himself chipped in with three. Yardley made 108 but Yorkshire lost their last seven wickets for 62 runs and their first-innings lead was a slender five runs.

It was now that Verity got to work. During the ten seasons of his first-class career which spanned the Thirties he took 1,956 wickets, 83 of them against Sussex at an average of 17.42. Opening the bowling at 12.15pm, he struck first ball when Parks was trapped lbw having elected to go up the order because Bob Stainton was nursing a leg injury. Verity's new ball partner, Ellis Robinson, had John Langridge taken at short leg and 12-2 quickly became 13-4 as Verity claimed Harry Parks and James Langridge in his third over.

Cox was now joined by Bartlett, who remembered Verity's remarkable performance: "The light billowing clouds of mist which often curled in from the sea at Hove were absent on the day of Hedley's last cricket triumph. There was a blazing sun and the wicket was ready for Hedley. It really suited him but you have got to be a good enough bowler to take advantage of it, which he did to our cost."

The wicket was cutting up badly as it dried out. Bartlett, Holmes and Griffith – three of the four amateurs in the Sussex side – were soon out, all bowled by Verity. At 25-7 there was little hope for the county. Cox would later claim that he top-scored in both innings after making nine to add to his 198, but Harry Parks made the same score. The tail failed to wag and in just 11.3 overs the innings was over – Sussex all out for 33, Verity finishing with 7-9 from six overs with one maiden.

"Verity bewildered, confused and confounded the enemy so completely that no batsman had time or opportunity to make double figures," wrote Kilburn. "The wicket was perfectly suited to spin bowling but the Sussex batsmanship was of the feeblest."

There is no doubting the quality of Verity's craft, but Jim Parks junior believes that for the first time in the match Sussex minds, inevitably given the circumstances, were elsewhere.

He says: "Dad always talked about Hedley Verity in glowing terms but that match was played in quite a surreal background. It's amazing that they played at all in the circumstances but they wanted to give Dad the chance to make a few quid."

Verity seldom courted publicity or tried to elicit praise for his endeavours on the cricket field although he seems to have been aware of the significance of the match, if not necessarily his performance in it. "I took the congratulations of the Sussex players, but I wondered if I would ever bowl at Hove again," he said.

There was a last twist as Yorkshire set out to score 29 for victory. Hutton needed seven runs to beat his previous best aggregate for a season of 2,888 runs set in 1937, but made just a single. The champions nonetheless gained their 20th victory of the season just after 2.30pm by nine wickets.

An hour or so later the Yorkshire players were back on their Southdown motor coach and heading home, Kilburn among the passengers.

"There was no guessing precisely what the future held, but there was no escaping the reflection that a much-loved way of life was being shattered, perhaps beyond repair," he wrote. "Scarcely anyone mentioned the cricket, though the past few days had brought cricket of uncommon quality.

"We reached the outskirts of the capital and for a mile or two the route led down the Great West Road towards London. In that direction there was no other traffic but the opposite path was crowded to danger point with every conceivable kind of vehicle carrying every conceivable cargo. Coach-loads of children swept to unknown foster homes. Urgency covered the earth."

At 6pm, barely four hours after Verity had spun Yorkshire to victory, Germany invaded Poland. Because of an experimental night-time blackout the Yorkshire players stopped for the night at Leicester but continued their journey soon after dawn. "Finally came journey's end in Leeds City Square," wrote Kilburn. "Thence departed their several ways one of the finest county teams in the history of cricket. It never assembled again."

Bill Bowes recalled how that Friday night he had spent long hours discussing the prospect of war with Verity and what they should do. In the end both joined up. Bowes took part in the North Africa campaign as a gunnery officer, Captain Verity accepted a commission into the Green Howards regiment.

In July 1943 he was seriously wounded by mortar fire during an attack on enemy positions in Catania on the island of Sicily. Captured by the Germans, he was treated for his wounds and then handed over to the Italians at the military hospital in Naples. An operation to remove part of his rib which was pressing down on his lung was successful but he died on 31st July 1943.

There was a poignant post-script to Verity's last wickets at Hove. In the first match of the opening post-war season in 1946 Yorkshire captain Brian Sellers put his hand into the top pocket of the blazer he had last worn at Hove nearly seven years earlier and picked out a tiny slip of paper. "Good God Norman, look at this," he said to Yardley. It was the scorer's chit, handed to him by Yorkshire scorer Billy Ringrose at Hove on 1st September 1939. The figures were faded but still legible. They recorded Verity's final bowling analysis – 6-1-9-7.

Two days after Verity had spun Yorkshire to victory Jim was at his grandmother's to hear Neville Chamberlain's fateful midday broadcast to the nation that Britain was at war with Germany. As father and son walked home in the late-summer sunshine they heard the air-raid sirens for the first time. For the next six years there would be no competitive cricket. The Second World War robbed great players of some of the best years of their career. Some, like Verity, made an even bigger sacrifice.

Jim senior was 36 when war was declared and, like Verity, probably knew that he had just played his last game of county cricket. He moved to Lancashire on police service and began playing in the Lancashire League for Accrington and in the Northern League for Blackpool, both competitions having carried on despite the hostilities. Jim could look back on a Sussex career which brought him 19,720 runs, the best 197 against Kent in 1936, and 795 wickets. Between 1927 and 1939 he passed 1,000 runs on 12 occasions.

When his playing days were over he moved to Trent Bridge to become Nottinghamshire coach and even at the age of 54 was playing second XI cricket. But in 1963 he returned to Hove as Sussex coach before a stroke forced him to retire, although he remained a regular visitor to the County Ground before his death in 1980.

Apart from Lord's, nowhere was wartime cricket played more regularly than Hove. In 1942 there were usually games on Wednesdays and Saturdays and with service teams using the County Ground frequently some of the greats of the world game enjoyed the welcome distraction of a game by the seaside, including Keith Miller, Denis Compton, Alf Gover, Gubby Allen and Trevor Bailey.

On one occasion during a match between the Home Guard, who were stationed at the County Ground, and a Sussex XI to raise money for the Spitfire Fund, Spen Cama – whose generosity after his death funded the redevelopment of Sussex's headquarters 80 years later – John Langridge, Maurice Tate and Arthur Gilligan were among those who ignored two air raid sirens to play on.

Only when a German bomber banked and scattered two bombs on the ground did they finally run for the shelters. One landed on the old squash club, the other in the south-east corner of the ground. Neither device exploded. That determination to carry on the game, so evident in late August 1939, had prevailed again.

JAMES KIRTLEY

2006: *"Everything felt just right"*

IN THE LIFE of a professional sportsman there are few occasions on the day of a game when he or she will wake up and feel everything is just right. No aches and pains, no mental anguish about what might lie ahead later in the day. Instead, the body feels energised and the mind is relaxed. The only focus is doing your job and doing it well.

On the morning of Saturday 26th August 2006, James Kirtley woke up in his hotel bedroom a few hundred yards from Lord's cricket ground in just such a contented frame of mind. Later that day he would be part of the first Sussex team to play in a one-day final at headquarters for 13 years. In most players such an occasion would understandably leave them feeling nervous and apprehensive. It certainly affected quite a few of his team-mates when the Cheltenham & Gloucester Trophy final against Lancashire began, but not Kirtley.

"The day before I bowled well in the nets on the Nursery Ground and felt good," he remembers. "Then on the morning of the game we had a warm-up game of football and I scored a goal which was practically unheard of because I was useless at football and didn't like the kick-about we used to have to get ourselves warmed up. I was always worried that I would pick up a silly injury or someone else would.

"I bowled in the nets and our fielding coach, Richard Halsall, was taking the ball with the mitt behind the stumps and the ball was just flying through. Physically I felt good. There were no aches and pains, which was extremely rare as any fast bowler will tell you, and I honestly thought I could not have been better prepared. Moments like that were very rare in my career and I guess that's the same for most pro sportsmen. I just felt right. Everything was in place that day right from the minute I walked to the ground from the hotel and saw all of the Sussex supporters."

Kirtley was always regarded as a quite intense character, both by team-mates and opponents. Now, two years after he ended a 15-year career which included 16 appearances for his country, he admits that he often struggled to really enjoy the good times. There were a lot as well, far more than most county cricketers can expect. He was man of the match on his England Test debut and was part of the most successful Sussex side in the long and quite often inglorious history of the oldest of the first-class counties.

But that overcast, damp Saturday morning felt different and Kirtley's belief that this might turn out to be a very good day was not misplaced. Shortly after 6pm he was cavorting around the boundary at Lord's with the rest of his team-mates after taking 5-27 – the best bowling figures in a one-day final – as Sussex pulled off the unlikeliest of victories over their old rivals in what is regarded as one of the great one-day games at Lord's.

Kirtley's celebration after he took the wicket of Murali Kartik to wrap up victory remains ingrained in the memory of anyone who witnessed it. He sunk to his knees, arms aloft, before being buried under a pile of delighted team-mates.

Months of pent-up emotion were released in that moment. A few months earlier Kirtley was close to quitting the game altogether after he was suspended for an illegal bowling action. His determination to, in effect, clear his name and return to competitive action, culminating in that unforgettable afternoon at Lord's, has made that final the favourite memory of so many people who were part of Sussex's period of success, including Kirtley himself. And during the first decade of the new century they were spoiled for choice.

Doubts about the legality of his bowling action had been raised before, ironically when he should have been enjoying one of the best moments of his career. In 2001 Kirtley was chosen for a five-match one-day tour of Zimbabwe, a deserved reward for his consistent performances for his county since making his debut six years earlier. Taking the new ball with Matthew Hoggard in the series opener in Harare, Kirtley picked up two wickets. But his action aroused the suspicion of match referee Naushad Ali. Instead of expressing his concerns to the ICC Ali revealed his misgivings instead to an English journalist and suddenly there was a story. Ali eventually submitted a report to the ICC but not until the fourth match of the series had been played. The England management were unconcerned and played Kirtley in two of the subsequent matches, but he was ordered to take remedial action in the winter of 2001/02 with England's bowling coach Bob Cottam and his own county coach Peter Moores.

By the time Kirtley's action came under scrutiny again in the summer of 2005 he had gone on to play four Test matches and eight more one-day internationals. As Sussex were closing in on their first Championship title in 2003 they were given even more cause for celebration when Kirtley took 6-34 in the second innings at Trent Bridge as England beat South Africa. The harshest of spotlights – international competition – was on Kirtley again but when he toured Sri Lanka with England the following winter ICC match referee Clive Lloyd went out of his way to reassure Kirtley.

"I can understand that it has been hard for James Kirtley. I was a cricketer and I understand the guy's position," said Lloyd. "Nothing has been reported so Mr Kirtley can rest assured and so can the England team that everything is fine. The young guy has had some problems before. He has rectified his action and if as such things changed then we would take it from there but at the moment everything is alright."

The problem resurfaced in 2005. While Sussex were getting their annual thrashing at Edgbaston – a ground where they last won in 1982 – Warwickshire coach John Inverarity was supervising filming of Kirtley's action from several different angles. The umpires, David Constant and Barrie Leadbeater, were far from happy with Warwickshire's covert operation and when they discovered what had gone on Sussex captain Chris Adams was incandescent with rage. Nonetheless, having watched the footage, Constant and Leadbeater, two of the most respected umpires on the circuit, felt duty-bound to report Kirtley to the ECB.

On 17th October 2005 the governing body announced that after exhaustive testing Kirtley's elbow extension exceeded the permitted 15 degrees. To save his career he would have to go months of exhaustive remodelling of his action. In effect, he had to learn to be a fast bowler all over again.

"The second time I had to remodel my action was a lot harder than the first,"he remembers. "It wasn't private anymore – the first time it went under the radar a bit, but the second time was very public especially with the way Warwickshire had filmed me in secret."

Kirtley returned to the Indoor School at Hove to work with his coach Mark Robinson and, on four occasions, England's new bowling coach Troy Cooley. For the first few weeks all he experienced was frustration, as Robinson remembers: "It was a tough few months for James and a real eye-opener for me as his coach. We have good days and bad days and sometimes it was a case of one step forward and two back.

"But we had to do it properly and work through it because the consequences were huge. James could have ended up getting banned for 12 months and that was the last thing anybody wanted.

"I remember having two pictures on my computer, one of James with 11 degrees of movement – which was legal – and one of 19 degrees, which was not. I showed them to our coaching staff and (captain) Chris Adams but no one could spot the difference."

At his lowest point, in November 2005, Kirtley gave serious thought to giving up. But the thought of retiring with a stigma still attached to his name was too much to contemplate.

"I didn't achieve a lot for the first three months of that winter even though I worked extremely hard," he said. "The support I received from the club was fantastic and without it I might have packed it up. But I had finished the 2005 season with 104 wickets, more than any other year in my career, and if I'd retired then it would not have been on my terms and I didn't want that. People would have thought the worst and the stigma that I retired because I was unable to clear my name would have been with me for a long time. At the time, though, retiring was definitely the easy option."

The 15 degrees of movement now allowed was 50% more than when Kirtley had first been reported four years earlier. In February 2006 his remodelled action underwent stringent scrutiny at Loughborough University. He bowled six bouncers, six yorkers and six slower balls – all filmed on a camera which broke down his action into 25 frames per second. Kirtley had cut his run-up to 12 paces, a third less than before, but his efforts paid off. A few weeks later he was told he could resume his career.

The hard work, though, had only just started. Although Sussex were delighted that he had cleared his name Kirtley still had some way to go before he convinced Adams and Robinson that he was ready to play again. There was no doubt that his action looked a lot purer and finally he had been able to silence the doubters. But was he able to bowl with the same effectiveness as before?

Initially at least Sussex had misgivings when the 2006 season got underway. While Kirtley worked on his new action in a second-team game Duncan Spencer, an injury-prone quick whom Viv Richards claimed was the fastest bowler he had ever faced during Spencer's first spell in England with Kent, was signed on a short-term contract. Spencer made his debut at Hove against Warwickshire and took the first wicket of the 2006 season before quietly fading from the scene.

Kirtley returned to first-team duty in the opening match of the C&G Trophy at a gloomy Oval on 30th April but when James Benning hit him for four boundaries in an over early in his spell he might have wished he had continued his rehabilitation in the second team. Thanks to a brilliant 89 from Goodwin and Yardy's unbeaten 98, Sussex won their first game in the South Conference, the 18 counties plus Ireland and Scotland having been split along geographical lines with the two group winners progressing to the final.

Kirtley played again the following day in the win over Middlesex at Hove but it wasn't until Sussex's third group game against Glamorgan at Sophia Gardens in Cardiff that he felt he was hitting his straps. "I don't think anyone expected me just to come back and – bang – start taking wickets like I used to," he said.

That game would be remembered for a devastating spell by Pakistani Rana Naved, who took 5-30, but it was a significant milestone for his new-ball partner too. "The first time that everything felt natural was in that game," he recalled. "I got Robert Croft, who Glamorgan employed as a pinch-hitter, with the new ball and that felt great. Getting wickets at the end of an innings was never an issue for me. I could bowl averagely up front or in my second spell but I always had the ability to claw it back at the end. To bowl as well as I did that day, with the new ball, gave me a lot of confidence.

"Rana was a good influence for me that summer before he went off to play for Pakistan, who were touring England that year. We always bowled well in tandem and if you have a partner like him who has that wicket-taking ability it does relax you and take the pressure off a bit. The same applied to Jason Lewry in Championship cricket."

On 18th May Kirtley played his first red-ball cricket of the season when he captained the side in a rain-ruined match against Sri Lanka at Hove which was notable for Ollie

Rayner's achievement in becoming the first Sussex player for 86 years to score a hundred on his first-class debut for the county. Kirtley took one wicket in 31 overs but was happy enough with how he bowled on an unresponsive pitch.

The season had started well for the county. They won four of their first five Championship games to lead the early table and further victories over Essex and Somerset put them firmly in control in their C&G Trophy group.

Kirtley probably owed his return to the Championship side for the game against Lancashire at Liverpool in early June to Rana's injury. The bowling honours went to Mushtaq Ahmed and Jason Lewry, who both took five wickets with Lewry claiming his 500th first-class victim. Kirtley was satisfied with his own performance and took the only wicket to fall in Lancashire's second innings as they wrapped up victory by nine wickets inside two days to stall Sussex's early momentum.

Rana was still sidelined when Sussex headed to the Clontarf Ground in Dublin to face Ireland in the C&G Trophy four days later. Instead of calling up a young bowler they gave Lewry a rare opportunity in one-day cricket that he took with two wickets. Kirtley, meanwhile, was hit for 20 in one of his overs although he finished with 3-46 as Sussex cantered to victory to set up what was effectively a semi-final against Hampshire at Hove on 16th June.

The County Ground was packed that Friday night despite the presence of the *SkyTV* cameras. Encounters between the two teams were always spicy when Adams and Shane Warne led the respective sides and this one was no different. For Kirtley, though, it was the first time that summer when he felt the hard work on his action really paid off.

He finished with 5-43, his most treasured victim that of the Hampshire captain who departed in a state of high dudgeon after being yorked off the first ball of the penultimate over.

The incident still makes Kirtley smile. "I was fielding on the boundary and Jim May, who was on the committee at the time before becoming chairman, walked past me and said something to the effect that it would be appreciated if I could knock Warney's stumps over," he says. "There might have been an expletive used before the word stumps.

"Anyway, I bowled him and turned to Jim and gave him the thumbs-up. The crowd loved it but Warney thought I was giving him a send-off and he started to walk towards some of the boys rather than the pavilion. I think he claimed afterwards that he had lost his bearings."

Thanks to an unbeaten 69 by Carl Hopkinson, Sussex knew exactly where they were heading. They won the game by five wickets and had secured their first Lord's final appearance since 1993.

The final was more than two months away. Enough time for anyone to suffer a slump in form and a week before Lord's Kirtley was riddled with self-doubt. He says: "My form took a bit of a dip and a few days prior to the final I wasn't even sure that I would be involved."

In the meantime, Sussex had failed to progress to the knockout stages of the Twenty20 Cup, despite their consistent form in the 50 overs competition. They won four of their eight group games but managed to maintain their Championship challenge and Kirtley took only his fourth wicket of the four-day season on 14th July against Kent when he uprooted Martin van Jaarsveld's off stump at Hove. That game ended in a draw and Kirtley was left out in favour of a second spinner in the next match at Southgate which also ended in a draw with Middlesex nine wickets down in their second innings.

Hard to believe now, as cricket fans ponder the dog's breakfast that is the fixture list these days, but six years ago there was actually some order to the schedule. The 50-over and 20-over competition group stages were finished and on 25th July Sussex began their Pro40 League campaign with a Division One fixture against Warwickshire.

With Adams recovering from a badly bruised thumb Kirtley captained the side and bowled well, taking 3-30 in an easy win. It was a significant show of support given that he had resigned the vice-captaincy at the start of the season to concentrate on bowling. Four wickets in the Championship game at Edgbaston which followed represented Kirtley's best performance with the red ball so far that season but with Yasir Arafat now installed as second overseas player, he was left out of the crucial home game against Lancashire which the visitors saved on the last day thanks to an unbeaten hundred from Mal Loye.

The following day Adams made a blistering 132 not out off 101 balls against the same opponents – the 20th hundred of his one-day career – but in a stop-start season Kirtley's form was beginning to suffer. He did remove Nathan Astle and Stuart Law but his eight overs went for 55 runs.

"Being made captain against Warwickshire in our first Pro40 game gave me some belief and I bowled well but against Lancashire I got smashed all over the place," says Kirtley.

"The following week we played Essex, again at Hove, and I bowled five overs for 48 runs. Jason Lewry had started picking up the white ball again and the feeling at the time was that we were struggling to pick up early wickets in one-day cricket, something Jason had the knack of doing throughout his career. If you can get two or three early wickets in a one-day game I have always believed it made things so much easier as a fielding side. I had bowled poorly in the two games leading up to the final and a week before I wasn't sure I would be playing."

In the build-up to their last game before the final, against Glamorgan at Hove six days prior to Lord's, there was fevered speculation that both Lewry and Kirtley would both play and effectively have their own bowl-out. But Lewry, although named in the squad, was left out, and Kirtley knew – injury permitting – that he would be taking the new ball against Lancashire.

He says: "I bowled well against Glamorgan (2-22 from six overs) and got it back a bit. It might have been the last-chance saloon for me but the management backed me and that was a massive lift. I played in a couple of Championship games and I was around the team a lot more leading-up to the final. To know I was playing was a huge relief."

Kirtley was used to playing in front of big crowds but for most of his team-mates it was a new experience. "Just being part of an occasion like that, with nearly 24,000 people in the ground, made me feel good before the game started," he recalls.

His sense of wellbeing was heightened by his record at headquarters. He had taken 49 wickets at Lord's for Sussex while one of the highlights of his career had come there in 2002 when he took what is considered to be one of the finest ever catches there, a sensational one-handed take with his weaker left-hand during a one-day international against India, his only international appearance at the home of the game.

"Lord's was a good ground for me and I always bowled well from the Nursery End. If ever I wasn't bowling particularly well I'd get a bit crossed and my front foot would come over towards the stumps more and I wouldn't be able to get through my action.

"But with the slope at Lord's I was able to line myself up a lot better and get through the crease."

With low clouds scudding across NW8 and rain in the air Kirtley was desperate to bowl first, especially as the sun was forecast to come out later in the day. Lord's had been good to batsmen that summer but there was always assistance for bowlers on the first day of Championship games, although no one could have predicted the final would be such a low-scoring contest.

Adams and Mark Chilton went out to toss after a short shower which delayed the start for 15 minutes. "It's funny because I was so convinced we had won the toss and would be bowling. I saw Grizz go out with Chilton and I started putting on my bowling boots," said Kirtley. "I think it was Carl Hopkinson who said to me 'what are you doing?' I said 'we're bowling aren't we?' Conditions for bowling were perfect. I always liked bowling first and during my Sussex career I always felt when we put sides in in one-day cricket we were successful because we were good at containing."

Kirtley may have been feeling calm but some of his team-mates were clearly betrayed by nerves.

In the third over Richard Montgomerie was run out for one after a brilliant stop and throw by Tom Smith in the covers. Matt Prior attacked impressively but in the eighth over he mis-timed a pull off Kyle Hogg and Sussex were 27-2.

It got worse. Adams was nearly involved in two run-outs before he was caught at second slip and Goodwin soon followed. Sussex had lost the cream of their batting for 46 runs and only six runs were added before Hopkinson caught the prevailing mood, attempting a reckless run to mid-on where Dominic Cork's direct hit left him well short of his ground and Sussex 52-5.

Kirtley watched all this with a growing sense of unease from the balcony in front of the home dressing room. He says: "I knew there were a lot of nerves when Monty got run out. Normally he was such a consistently calming presence in our side but even he looked under pressure. Hoppo's run-out was another sign of it and there were one or two bad shots. It wasn't good to watch."

As Kirtley started rooting in his bag for his batting gear, Robin Martin-Jenkins began to counter-attack before he was controversially given out caught behind to a big nip-backer from Glen Chapple which TV replays showed hit neither bat or glove. His father Christopher, commentating in the *BBC* radio box in the media centre, did his best to maintain a sense of equilibrium but at 78-6 he, like the rest of the Sussex supporters, was fearing the worst. The bookmakers pushed the odds of a Sussex win out to 16-1.

Arafat came out to join Mike Yardy and in their contrasting styles the pair began to restore some confidence in Sussex ranks. Their half-century partnership came in 45 minutes and while Yardy, whose only boundary was a nick through the slips, was happy to accumulate in ones and twos his partner played attractively until Sajid Mahmood returned to the attack and soon had him caught behind for 37. Nonetheless a stand of 56 had helped to lift the mood. Yardy was eighth out in the 43rd over, also for 37 but Wright plundered 19 off 19 balls and Mushtaq Ahmed hit a couple of nice shots before he was last out in the 48th over. Sussex had somehow cobbled together 172 from the ruins of 78-6.

Kirtley remembers the dressing room mood improving as the lower-order hit back. He says: "Yards and Yasir gave us some momentum and then Luke took the attack back to them and Mushy played a couple of cheeky shots. So we knew we had a chance but we also realised that winning a game from this position would be a real one-off. At halfway Lancashire were in control. We had fought back a bit and we knew we had an opportunity if we could take early wickets but you couldn't say the game was in the balance – far from it in fact."

Adams gathered his players together in the dressing room before they went out to field and said to them, as Kirtley describes: "Nothing that memorable – he just wanted us to do the basics well and keep believing in ourselves." When the players emerged the clouds had parted and Lord's was bathed in warm sunshine. The bookies felt slightly more optimistic about Sussex's chances but not much. They were now available at 10-1. "We knew there was still enough in the pitch that if we stayed disciplined in our bowling we could create pressure but we also realised we needed early wickets," says Kirtley.

It didn't start well for Kirtley. To the first delivery of the fifth over, Loye picked up a length ball outside off-stump and swung him high for a leg-side six that finished ten rows back in the Grandstand. "We had a man out there because we knew he would play that shot at some stage but it flew into the crowd over his head," recalls the bowler. The next ball was a wide. Lancashire voices were in full cry. Then the game changed.

Loye played down the wrong line to the next delivery which was full and straight. Kirtley's appeal had barely been answered in the affirmative when Loye turned to head back to the pavilion. He was walking. In a Lord's final.

Kirtley says: "I hardly saw that happen more than two or three times in my career but Mal was always a bit idiosyncratic. I think he knew he was plumb but it was still a surprise when he just trudged off. It was a big boost. Mal could have made a mockery of the chase if he'd got going."

In came the New Zealander Nathan Astle. Sussex had worked out when the teams had met earlier in the month in the Pro40 game that he was a vulnerable starter and in his next over, with a delivery which cut in off the seam, Kirtley trapped him leg before.

The next man in was Stuart Law, who loved nothing more than pounding the Sussex bowlers. For Essex and Lancashire he had scored 11 hundreds against the county including two in one-day cricket. His was the wicket coveted more than anyone else by Adams and his team.

"Law had been a thorn in our side throughout my career," said Kirtley. "But we knew if we could get him early we had a chance." No one could quite believe how early. Kirtley's first ball to the Queenslander was ramrod straight and when it thudded into his pads up went Kirtley and the close-catchers, followed by several thousand Sussex voices in the stands. After what seemed like an eternity, umpire Jeremy Lloyds slowly raised his finger. Lancashire were 27-3 and in the space of 13 balls Kirtley had single-handedly dragged his side back into the game. Who cared that as he walked back shaking his head TV replays showed that Law had got an inside edge.

Kirtley says: "When I appealed I was convinced he was out. I never heard the inside edge and I doubt if the umpire had either. I'd just got Astle so the noise levels were up and the adrenalin was pumping." For Sussex there was a sense of justice served, Martin-Jenkins having been on the end of a poor umpiring decision earlier in the day.

At the end of the over Kirtley returned to the deep and hundreds of Sussex supporters in the Edrich and Compton stands rose to acclaim him and he now recalls: "My heart was pounding and I knew I needed to calm down and take some deep breaths. It's funny, but it was only when I looked at the game again on DVD that I got an idea of the reception from our supporters. At the time I was just so focused it barely registered."

Kirtley would normally take a breather after four overs with the new ball. Adams wisely kept him on for another two and when he came off he had figures of 6-1-17-3 including that six by Loye.

Adams made a double change, bringing on Martin-Jenkins in the 12th over and then Wright. Martin-Jenkins soon settled into an immaculate line and length but Wright looked nervous. His first over cost ten runs as he struggled for rhythm but in his second over extra pace gave Luke Sutton the hurry-up and he mishit a pull to mid-on. Lancashire were 51-4 and for the first time Sussex were favourites.

Mushtaq Ahmed replaced Wright at the Nursery End and Adams bravely kept attacking with a slip and silly point. Chapple relieved some of the tension by striking the leg-spinner for two boundaries before Mushtaq used all his experience to end Chilton's dogged resistance, which had lasted for 93 minutes. In the 23rd over he sensed the batsman coming down the pitch and fired a googly down the leg side which Chilton had only a slim chance chance of hitting or smothering with his pad. He did neither and when Prior whipped off the bails Chilton was well out of his ground and the score was 67-5.

Chapple then prodded at a googly and Montgomerie dived to take a brilliant tumbling catch at silly point. Halfway through their reply Lancashire were 72-6.

Kirtley recalls: "Mushy and Robin came on and bowled outstandingly, Wrighty bounced out Sutton, Chilton was stumped off a wide and then Monty took that amazing catch. We just kept chipping away." Martin-Jenkins and Mushtaq had combined figures of 2-45 from 19 overs and their contribution to the victory should never be forgotten.

If Law had often been Sussex's nemesis over the years then Dominic Cork was not far behind. Adams and Cork had once been Derbyshire team-mates but there was no love lost between them now. Only a few weeks earlier Cork had defied the pain of a split finger by batting for an hour to help save the Championship game at Hove. On a couple of occasions the pair nearly collided and there was much comical glaring and grimacing. It was hard to discern whether two old stagers were hamming it up or if there really was an edge. Kirtley knew, though, that Cork was the master of the backs-to-the-wall fight.

Kirtley says: "I still remember when he defied Courtney Walsh and Curtly Ambrose to win a Test match for England at Lord's so we knew he wouldn't give it up. When he came in he was quite quiet which was unusual for Corky. He knew he was up against it but he'd been there before."

In Tom Smith, Cork found a reliable partner and slowly the momentum started to shift. Cork hit Martin-Jenkins for a couple of boundaries to spoil his figures and soon they had a fifty partnership. With ten overs to go Lancashire needed 51 runs with four wickets in hand. It was anyone's game.

It was now that Kirtley and Arafat used all their experience to keep Cork off strike and tried to attack at the other end. They both returned briefly to the attack and then in the 42nd over Adams turned to Wright. Hogg immediately mistimed a drive and the ball looped towards mid-on. Montgomerie was almost on his knees to take the catch but despite getting both hands on the ball it rolled onto the turf. Montgomerie looked mortified but redemption was only a minute or so away.

In keeping with a day when a lot of batsmen played with scrambled senses, Hogg attempted an identical shot four balls later. This time Montgomerie hung on and Lancashire were 130-7, Hogg and Cork having added 58 which was the highest stand of the match.

"We all bowled well to Corky," remembers Kirtley. "The pitch was to the right of centre looking from the pavilion slightly towards the Tavern side. We kept bowling into his pads and allowing him to take a single so we could attack the other batsmen. We knew Corky would hang around but after Hogg got out it was a case of whether anyone would stay with him long enough."

Smith tried to and together they knocked 21 runs off the target, mostly in singles. Adams summoned Kirtley at the Pavilion End for the 46th over. Kirtley recalls: "It was getting very tense by then. They needed 22 to win and Corky was relishing the situation. But again I felt great. I knew the enormity of the situation of course, but I still felt very calm about things."

With his third ball Kirtley pinned Smith with a classic nip-backer. With only Mahmood – who could be hit or miss – and Murali Kartik to come Cork began to take singles he might otherwise have turned down. He was relishing the situation but the pressure got too much for his partner. Off the last ball of the 47th over, Mahmood had a head-in-the-air mow at a straight ball from Arafat and lost his middle stump, and it was 156-9.

For the 48th over Adams spread the field, allowing Cork who was on strike to take an easy single. Kartik had no pretensions as a batsman but his one-day average of 10.99 wasn't the worst for a number 11. From the first ball of the over Cork took a single off Kirtley and Kartik was on strike. The next delivery nipped back off the pitch and thudded into Kartik's pads. Neil Mallender slowly raised his finger and Sussex joy was unconfined.

Kirtley had never been one for flamboyant celebrations. Throughout his career a simple high-five with the nearest team-mate was often enough but not this time. He sank to his knees, fists clenched and for a couple of precious seconds savoured what he had achieved before being submerged under a scrum of blue shirts. Nine months after he had almost given up the game he was enjoying the best moment of his Sussex career.

He recalls: "That celebration was just an outpouring of different emotions that had been building up for the previous nine months – mostly joy, some relief but also some anger. There were tears and I suppose two fingers up to a few people as well. I did feel vindicated.

"I had bowled with a good, high action and taken five wickets in a Lord's final. It wasn't classic Kirtley firing in yorkers and slower balls all the time. It was holding length and getting lbws which was an unusual one-day performance for me."

A few minutes later Kirtley was getting his hands on the big silver trophy and carrying it around the boundary edge as thousands of Sussex supporters savoured a moment only the grey-beards among them had witnessed before. Forty-three years after Ted Dexter had led the county to victory in the first-ever one-day final Sussex were winners at Lord's for the fifth time.

Kirtley and his captain were whisked off to do a round of press interviews and it was another hour before they returned to the dressing room where Adams gathered his players together to pay an emotional tribute to each and every one of them. When he got around to his match-winner Kirtley was struggling to hold back the tears.

A few hours later, as the celebrations continued in the team hotel, the sheer physical and emotional effort finally took its toll on the man of the match. "I just hit the wall – I was done in. And we had a five-hour coach trip to Durham the next day for a Pro40 game as well," he says.

Six years on and the memories of that Lord's day are still crystal-clear. And if he does need reminding Kirtley will often dust off the DVD and watch it again, often with his young son Ollie for company. He still has the match ball duly mounted and the shirt he wore was donated to the Sussex museum.

Kirtley says: "It was such a great time to play for Sussex and I was very fortunate to be part of it. Between 2003 and 2007 we won the Championship three times and did the double in 2006 but that was undoubtedly my best moment for Sussex.

"I didn't play when we won the Championship for the first time in 2003 because I had been with England. Don't get me wrong, that was a great moment but with everything else that happened to me afterwards that game at Lord's almost felt like my thank-you to everyone who had supported me.

"By that stage of my career I knew I wasn't going to play much for England anymore (he did play once in the 2007 Twenty20 World Cup) and my focus was to win games for Sussex and to enjoy myself. When we won trophies it felt more gratifying. It's not that I didn't enjoy our earlier success, but I didn't always allow it to be a fun thing because I was always trying to get to the next level."

Kirtley did retire on his own terms. In September 2010 he took his bow at a packed Hove for the last time and fittingly perhaps his final wicket was Kevin Pietersen, arguably the best England batsman of his generation. It was a wonderful piece of cricketing theatre but nothing will ever beat that August day at Lord's when Kirtley found redemption and gave a generation of Sussex supporters a day they will always remember.

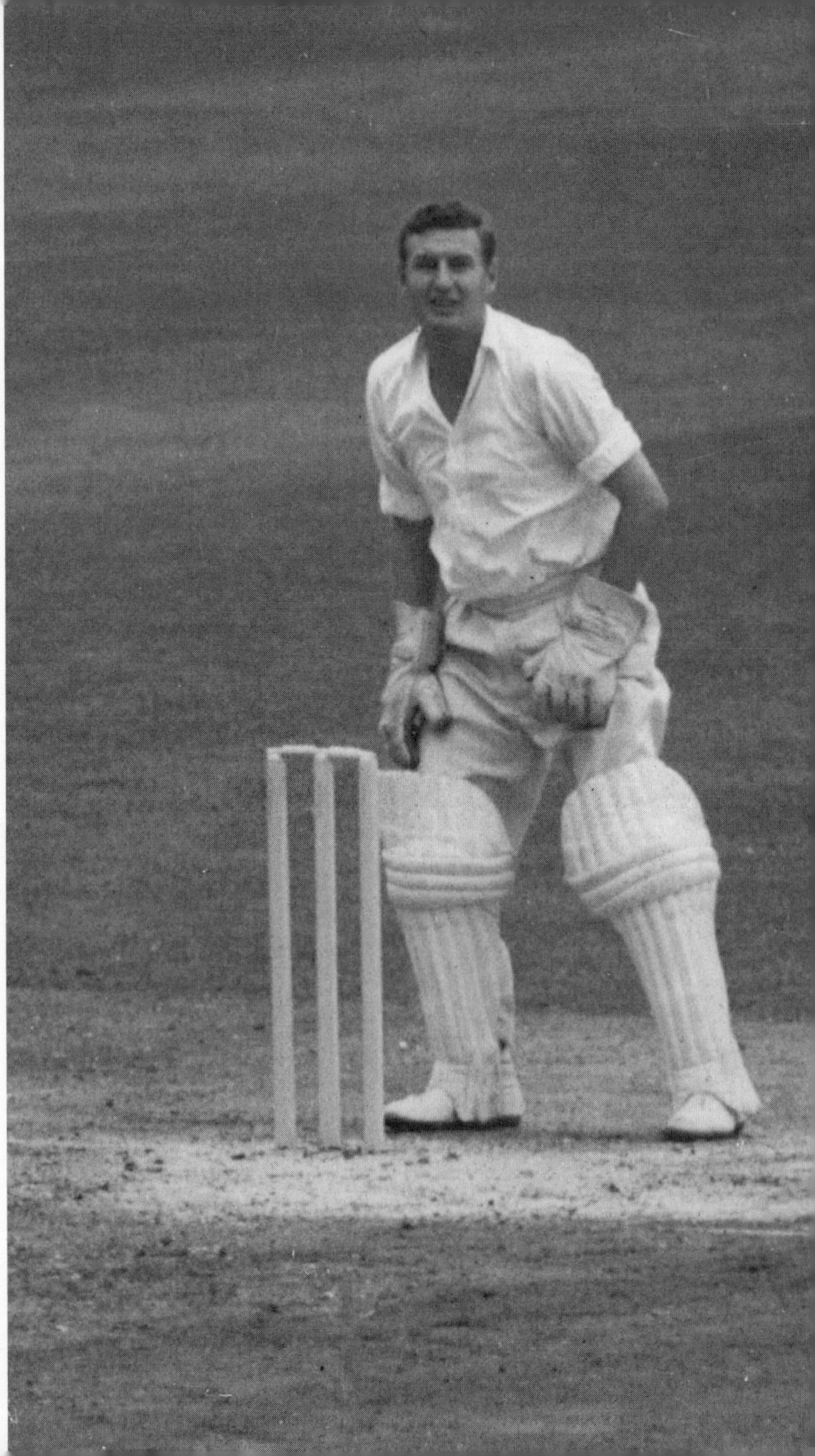

JIM PARKS JNR

1963: One-Day Pioneers

JIM PARKS IS unequivocal in his assessment. I've just asked him to compare the Sussex team which won the domestic game's first one-day trophy 49 summers ago to the one which won four limited-overs prizes in four seasons between 2006 and 2009. Jim ruminates over his response for a few seconds. "Well, I think we might have just beaten them," he smiles.

His assessment is certainly not intended as a slight on Chris Adams, James Kirtley, Mushtaq Ahmed, Mike Yardy, Robin Martin-Jenkins and co. Jim was as proud as any Sussex man when the county won at Lord's for the first time in 20 years in 2006, defeating Lancashire in the final of the C&G Trophy, and followed it with back-to-back triumphs in the Pro40 League and a memorable Twenty20 win at Edgbaston in 2009.

"I just don't think the one-day sides back in the early 1960s perhaps got enough credit," he said. "A lot of very fine English players took to the one-day game very easily when it started, it's just there wasn't a lot of fuss made at the time. If we'd had a World Cup back then instead of waiting until 1975 I'm convinced England would have won it and probably the next one as well. It's just that in those days the one-day game didn't have anywhere near the profile it has now." The 1964 *Wisden* devoted just four haughty sections to its overall assessment of the embryonic one-day competition, two paragraphs on the final and the scorecards.

Nor was there much in terms of financial rewards. The players' bonus for beating Worcestershire in the first Gillette Cup final at Lord's in 1963 was a princely £25 while Sussex picked up £1,889 as winners. And they celebrated by watching the *Black and White Minstrel Show* at the Victoria Palace Theatre in London.

Jim still enjoys watching one-day cricket at Hove. He recognises the force for good that Twenty20 has been for the domestic game since it started in 2003 in terms of attracting a new audience into cricket grounds and providing a financial fillip for both the clubs themselves and the players, the most talented of whom can earn untold riches playing this form of the game all over the world now.

He laughs when asked to compare the one-day cricket of 1963 with the game being played nearly five decades later. "It's like black and white compared to colour," he smiled. "Back then the players just looked upon it as another game."

There was, at least, a reluctant realisation among the game's governors at Lord's that something needed to be done to liven up domestic cricket. 1963 may have marked the height of the Swinging Sixties but county cricketers had only just stopped coming onto the field from separate gates, when the distinction between amateurs and professionals came to an end in 1962. Finances were dwindling and players did not earn much for their six-days-a-week summer occupation and were seldom employed by the counties during the winter.

In 1963 Sussex's home programme of 16 first-class matches drew a total attendance of 42,000, an average of less than 3,000 a match for three-day games. A year later that aggregate had dipped to 36,000. The halcyon post-war days when crowds flocked to county cricket in their thousands were becoming a distant memory and most counties were feeling the pinch.

MCC had noted the success of the Rothmans International Cavaliers, who had been founded by Bagnall Harvey, an impresario and agent who had looked after the affairs of Denis Compton and turned him into someone recognised beyond just cricket followers. Compton effectively became English cricket's first poster boy in the post-war years thanks to sponsorship and endorsements arranged by Bagnall.

Among Bagnall's friends was Ted Dexter, England and Sussex captain. Bagnall found a sponsor – tobacco manufacturers Rothmans – who were interested in promoting regular one-day games on Sundays, the one day of the week which the average British worker took off at a time when six-days-a-week was still the norm in offices, shops and factories.

The BBC were interested in showing the matches, but only if they would finish at a certain time. It was a guarantee Bagnall could not give until Dexter showed the enlightened thinking that he was to replicate on the field when the one-day knockout began.

"You can," Dexter insisted. "You limit the overs and restrict the run-ups." Dexter wrote the rules and out of that the Rothmans International Cavaliers – cricket's equivalent of the Harlem Globetrotters – were born.

"Ted and I were always dashing off to play for the Cavaliers," said Jim. "It was great fun and there used to be some fantastic players involved. The crowds turned up in big numbers – they loved it because they could go along after Sunday lunch and still be home by 7pm. We'd play at a lot of club grounds and for a lot of people it was the first time they had seen some of the best players in the world. You have to remember that back then not a lot of people had TV and apart from the Tests there was very little cricket on television anyway."

Having noted the success of the Cavaliers, in 1962 MCC's cricket committee, whose members included Jim, gave the green light to the One-Day Knockout. Sponsorship was secured from Gillette, although they were seldom mentioned in the pre-publicity, and on 22nd May 1963 English cricket entered a brave new world when eight first-round ties took place, Lancashire having beaten Leicestershire in a rain-affected preliminary round tie to secure their progress into the last 16.

Jim wasn't alone in thinking that the competition would be a short-lived experiment. There was at least a consensus amongst the counties that something needed to be done to attract more spectator interest and Gillette's offer of £6,500 met with a favourable reaction.

"We loved the game, of course we did, and if you played Test cricket the rewards were there. But cricket was never going to make anyone wealthy," remembers Jim.

Dexter hated dull cricket. To liven up a moribund Championship game he would often declare early to set a tempting target or collude with his opposite number "to try and make a game of it". If his overtures were rejected he would quite happily leave Parks or another of the senior pros in charge and retire to the captain's room at Hove to listen to the horse-racing on the radio.

But he quickly realised that with their strong seam attack, a long batting order and good fielders, Sussex could be a force in the new format. Jim says: "We didn't do any specific practice for the first game but Ted did get us together and said 'Look, we're never going to win the Championship but with our attack and our batting we can win this. We will bat first if we win the toss. If we don't, you'll find the others will put us in. We will play properly for 20 or 30 overs then Parkser, (Ken) Suttle and Coops (Graham Cooper) would get the runs'."

He adds: "Ted grasped the nettle very quickly. I remember that first-round game against Kent at Tunbridge Wells. It was a good batting wicket and we were fortunate that year that we batted first in every game because Ted preferred to defend a target. In contrast to Ted, dear old Colin Cowdrey was still attacking with two slips and a gully in the 65th over.

"When we fielded we tended to start with a slip but not for long. Ted soon had everyone on the boundary. Our seam attack would bowl back-of-a-length which was difficult to score off and we always had a man in front of the wicket rather than at, say, second slip, to cut off the singles."

Sussex made 314-7, the highest total of the round, with Suttle underpinning the innings by scoring 104 when batting at number three. Jim made a sprightly 59 and Dexter added 45. Despite 127 from Peter Richardson, which won the Kent opener the £50 man of the match award, Sussex were victorious by 72 runs, Dexter employing his men on the boundary virtually from the start.

"Ted's idea was to keep wickets in hand for 30 overs and then have a go," said Jim. "We had a lot of guys who could hit the ball hard in our lower order. Les Lenham and I had a go at the end and in the last eight overs we scored a hundred runs. Even by today's standards with the big, heavy bats they have that isn't bad going at all."

The ease of their victory did not surprise Jim. "We had a lot of players in our side who were suited to one-day cricket," he said. "We had some good stroke-players like Alan Oakman, Kenny Suttle, Ted, of course, and Richard Langridge and guys down the order who could slog for want of a better description – Les, Graham Cooper and Tony Buss. We also had a fine seam attack. If you took our side in 1963 and 1964 and put it in the modern era they would have been hard to beat and we'd have loved a crack at Twenty20."

The Kent committee was furious at what they regarded as negative and unsporting tactics by Dexter and wrote a letter of complaint to Sussex along those lines. Dexter laughed it off. He knew this was the best chance the county had of finally ending their long wait for silverware. "We were there to win, not make friends," said Jim.

The players treated it as just another game according to Jim, admittedly a longer one than they were used to. Play didn't start until 11am and with lunch, tea and 130 overs to fit in matches would often finish in twilight, especially with captains reluctant to employ their spin bowlers. Not surprisingly, the competition's matches were reduced to 60 overs in 1964.

The Nevill Ground had been packed for the Kent game. The public clearly had an appetite for one-day cricket but Sussex were nonetheless taken aback by the size of the audience for the second-round match against Yorkshire at Hove three weeks later. More than 15,000 spectators paying

5/- (25 pence) shoehorned themselves in for an absorbing game which finished at 7.45pm with Sussex victorious by 22 runs and progressing to the semi-finals.

"I don't think I played in any better one-day game than the quarter-final against Yorkshire," remembers Jim. "The ground was packed. There were 15,000 inside and when you consider how relatively small the County Ground is you can get an idea how busy it was.

"Ted and I toured with England and were used to big crowds, particularly in places like India, but to a lot of the lads it was a bit of a shock. They just got on with it though."

Yorkshire had an outstanding side including Fred Trueman and Tony Nicholson – both experienced and highly skilled bowlers – with Trueman operating up the slope and conceding just 40 runs in his 14 overs.

"No bowler could bowl right through," said Jim. "You could bowl a maximum of 15 overs so most would bowl in two or three spells. And hardly any side had a spinner. Seamers gave you more control so most captains preferred all-seam attacks."

Sussex made 292 off 64 overs with Jim scoring a fluent 90 at number five after opener Langridge made 56 and Dexter 44. "It was a big total but they started off quicker than we had and for a while they looked like favourites."

Jim was in fine form that day. Sussex were 126-3 when he came in and the run rate needed to quicken. After taking just 70 minutes over his first 50 he took the attack apart, scoring 30 runs off his next eight balls. "I hit Tony Nicholson over extra cover a lot," he recalls. "The ball was coming on to the bat quickly and therefore went a bit finer. I hit two or three sixes over point off the front foot, one of which landed on the pavilion roof." Jim then hooked Mel Ryan for six, hitting a spectator, as he scored his last 40 in 15 minutes before Nicholson trapped him lbw for a magnificent 90.

A then-young Geoff Boycott remembers Jim's onslaught well. He said: "I had never seen anyone play like that. Tony would bowl mainly out-swingers with the odd nip-backer from the Sea End and Jim twice hit him inside out over extra cover into the pavilion. I'd grown up playing tough league cricket in Yorkshire on green wickets where you just didn't play shots like that. It was unbelievable to watch."

Yorkshire could bat deep as well and the turning point came when a bespectacled Boycott took on Ian Thomson in the deep.

"Geoff was only 22 and it was the first time I'd seen him play," remembers Jim. "Technically, I think he was the best batsman we produced since the Second World War and he had all the shots, especially in his younger days. He'd got to 71 and they needed 30 with two wickets in hand. He guided Tony Buss down to third man where Thommo, who was off balance, picked it up. He had a fantastic arm, I didn't have to move an inch to take the catch and whip the bails off with Geoff a yard short."

Jim caught Nicholson off Buss to complete the victory as Sussex got home by 22 runs, their success greeted by a mass pitch invasion of delighted schoolboys. With four catches to go with his runs, Jim was named man of the match and he shared the £50 among his team-mates.

Jim's form in one-day cricket was not reflected in Championship games. He only made one first-class century that summer – 136 against Kent in late July at Hastings where there were record gate receipts for the Central Ground of £1,400 – but his form with bat and gloves caught the eye of his captain, who was also leading England, and when Northamptonshire's Keith Andrew was dropped after the first Test against West Indies Jim was recalled to the England team for the second Test at Lord's after an absence of nearly three years.

Eight days after the victory over Yorkshire in the quarter-final, Jim found himself playing in what is still regarded as one of the best Test matches ever seen in this country. It reached a climax with two balls to go when Colin Cowdrey, his left arm broken earlier in the day and in a sling, went out to join David Allen with six runs wanted and one wicket needed by West Indies. Allen kept out Wes Hall to prevent England going two-down in the series.

Jim's contribution – 52 runs (35 and 17) and three second-innings catches – was tidy enough but he saw at first hand two of, in their own ways, the bravest Test innings ever played in England; Dexter's counter-attacking 70 off 73 balls in the first innings against a phenomenal West Indies' pace attack and Brian Close's second-innings 70 when he was peppered by Hall, Charlie Griffith and co and left black and blue with bruises.

Griffith got Jim out four times during the series and it didn't take long for Jim to join a long list of opponents deeply suspicious of his action. "He was a chucker, but he didn't chuck all of them," recalled Jim. "When he bowled properly he was medium pace and you could play him with one hand in your pocket. He chucked his bouncer, which was three or four yards quicker. When you chuck a ball it cuts and it rotates against the arm. At Lord's this bouncer bowled up the hill pitched and got underneath my bat, went between my upper arm and chest and through to the keeper."

England won the third Test at Edgbaston by 217 runs where Jim avoided losing his wicket to Griffith but only made 17 runs (12 and 5) and took three catches. Thanks to Freddie Trueman's 12 wickets, including 7-44 in the second innings, England headed to Headingley all-square in the series.

There Jim scored 22 and 57 – he made nine Test fifties and two centuries in 46 games – in the second innings on the fourth day when, despite the certainty of English defeat, a crowd of 20,000 turned up. Jim and Brian Close added 69 in 73 minutes before Jim was leg before to Lance Gibbs. He hit five fours and two sixes, one of which was carried over the boundary line by Joe Solomon.

The West Indies completed a 3-1 series win at the Oval in August where Jim and Dexter secretly filmed Griffith's action on an 8mm cine camera. A few weeks later they showed the footage to a selected audience at Hove including a couple of umpires who both agreed that Griffith's action was illegal. Jim felt vindicated even though impotent authorities both at Lord's and in the Caribbean did nothing about it. "There were more blatant chuckers than Charlie," says Jim, "But no one was as quick. With him you couldn't see the line, pick up the speed or bounce and defend yourself."

Even Griffith would have struggled to get much out of the wicket at Northampton where Jim and Sussex headed between the third and fourth Tests for the Gillette Cup semi-final. Having beaten two of the strongest counties in the country, Wantage Road held few fears for Dexter's men.

"We always fancied our chances up there," said Jim. "Ted made 115 (17 fours, one six) and we put on 160 together for the fourth wicket and then he took three wickets with his medium pace."

Jim's contribution to the partnership was 71 but there was a sensational finish to the Sussex innings when David Larter, no-balled by umpire Syd Buller five times earlier in the day for over-stepping, finished things off with a hat-trick. If only Buller had been a bit braver with Griffith in the Tests.

Northamptonshire's target was 293 and they never got close in drizzle and worsening light. Jim ran out Brian Reynolds with a direct hit, the dangerous Colin Milburn was dismissed for just six and although Roger Prideaux, who was to become a Sussex player, scored 73 Sussex's all-seam attack held sway. Thomson took 4-33 in 13.3 overs and when the game finished just before 8pm Dexter's men had won by 105 runs. Worcestershire, having bowled out Lancashire for just 59 in the other semi at New Road to set up a nine-wicket win, were to be their opponents in the final.

The final itself was still several weeks away and Sussex put thoughts of Lord's to one side. There was a Championship to be won and in mid-July, after recording their eighth victory of the summer, they led the table. But, clearly hindered by the absence of two of their best players who were with England, they won just twice more and in the week before the final they spent most of the time cooped up in the pavilion at Hastings, the three-day festival match against Arthur Gilligan's XI at the Central Ground abandoned without a ball bowled.

At least it gave Jim and the rest of the squad, which included John Snow for the first time in the competition, ample time to get to London on the day before the final, although they went straight to the hotel. There was no need to check on the wicket at Lord's. After a week's rain they knew the uncovered pitch would be damp.

Snow was beginning to make his mark in Championship cricket and his inclusion in the final XI was not that great a surprise. Bob Pountain, who had played against Kent and Northamptonshire, missed out. "To be honest, Bob didn't contribute to either win a great deal," recalled Jim. "We had to hide him in the field a bit because he wasn't the quickest on his feet."

Pountain would spend the following winter, when he should have been felling trees for the former Surrey captain Stuart Surridge, pedalling away on a static bike in the old Hove General Hospital in an effort to lose weight. He shed two and a half stone but the perception of him remained unchanged. Jack Arlidge, the doyen of the Hove press box, nicknamed him "Man-Mountain Pountain". Jim adds: "His real name was Francis, I never understood why he was called Bob."

When they arrived at Lord's the following morning Jim wasn't convinced there would be any cricket at all. The atmosphere was still damp but with a full house of 25,000 in the crowd the onus was on umpires Fred Gardner and Frank Lee to get the players out there. "It would never have started these days but I think the authorities felt we had to play," said Jim.

As well as Snow, Sussex employed spin for the first time in the competition. Alan Oakman's off-breaks were good enough to have brought him 51 wickets at 17.01 in the Championship that summer and he finished top of the county's bowling averages but it was with the bat that he made his first contribution, helping Langridge put on 62 for the first wicket.

The pitch was slow and Worcestershire's two left-arm spinners Norman Gifford and Doug Slade, backed up by Martin Horton's under-rated off breaks, were soon making inroads, slicing through Sussex's top and middle order. But Jim counter-attacked impressively as conditions began to ease and made 57 in 90 minutes, driving the ball handsomely to the delight of an increasingly vociferous contingent of Sussex supporters, most of whom were on the Tavern side of the ground. He hit a six and four fours.

Sussex eventually got to 168 with only Jim, the openers and Snow, who made ten batting at number ten, getting into double figures. Gifford's 4-33 in 15 overs earned him the Man of the Match award and Slade took 2-23 from 11. Horton finished with 1-20 from eight.

"It didn't appear to be enough but we were always confident," insists Jim. Whereas Worcestershire captain Don Kenyon had employed two slips, a gully and short leg Dexter went on the defensive from the start with just a slip for the opening bowlers Thomson and Buss. Dexter was going to make Worcestershire graft for every run.

The light got steadily worse as late afternoon turned to early evening. At 80-2 Worcestershire were in a strong position but then Oakman, bowling an impeccable length, had Tom Graveney caught by Dexter and from there on Worcestershire began to lose wickets regularly. Oakman's 13 overs cost just 17 runs and with the seamers providing excellent support at the other end Sussex strangled the life out of the reply.

"Oaky should have had Man of the Match that day," reckons Jim. "He kept Ron Headley quiet for more than two hours and then when Tom came in he had to up the tempo. He hit Oaky down to long on and there was Ted and Les Lenham going for the same ball. I remember Oaky shouting 'Captain!' because he had more confidence in Ted to take the catch and he caught it."

After Headley skied Don Bates to mid-on Snow was the sixth bowler employed by Dexter and, betraying any nerves he might have had, the son of a Bognor vicar had Bob Broadbent caught in the deep before bowling Gifford and Jack Flavell for ducks. "I remember seeing a picture of the Flavell dismissal in the paper the next day," said Jim. "It was so gloomy he could barely see the ball. The picture just shows him backing away and the middle stump flying out of the ground."

At 133-9 it looked all over but Jim's opposite number Roy Booth and last man Bob Carter decided to have some fun. They added 21, forcing Dexter to once again employ his fielders on the boundary. Carter was eventually run out and Sussex had won just before 7pm on a dank September evening by 14 runs.

"I always felt we would defend 168 even though it was less than three an over," said Jim. "The conditions didn't really improve all day and when the last wicket fell it was very gloomy."

As the trophy was held aloft by Dexter, the massed ranks of the Sussex faithful in the Tavern Stand raised their glasses in toast and the song Sussex by the Sea rang out.

The atmosphere set the tone for future one-day cup finals at headquarters although *Wisden* was somewhat sniffy in its assessment and wrote: "The new knockout competition aroused enormous interest. Very large crowds flocked to the matches and 25,000 watched the final at Lord's.

"At Lord's, supporters wore favours and banners were also in evidence, the whole scene resembling an association football Cup Final more than a game of cricket.

"Two points invited criticism: Firstly, the majority of counties were loath to include even one slow bowler and relied mainly on pace. Secondly, the placing of the entire field around the boundary to prevent rapid scoring – Dexter used this tactic in the final – became fairly common. The success of the spinners in the final may have exploded the first theory."

John Arlott, writing in the *Guardian*, was more enthusiastic. He said: "Perhaps it was not strictly speaking first-class cricket. But as entertainment it is with us for the foreseeable future and let us be grateful for it."

By the time Sussex had received the trophy and toasted their success in the dressing rooms it was getting on for 9pm. Nothing formal in the way of a celebration had been planned.

Jim remembered that Tony Mercer, who was directing the *Black and White Minstrel Show* at the Victoria Palace Theatre, had issued an open invitation to the Sussex players to come to the show were they to win.

"Tony was a big cricket fan and he told us if we won to come to the show," Jim says. "So we all piled into cabs and made our way down there. We'd had a few to drink by then and it was all a bit surreal. Halfway through the show they made this announcement that the winning Sussex team were in the audience and they invited us on stage and we got a fantastic ovation. I will never forget it."

By the end of the night most of the £25 bonus the players had received for winning the first silverware in Sussex's history had been spent.

Jim's aggregate of 277 competition runs placed him at the top of the first ever Gillette Cup averages. He made four half-centuries and averaged 69.25. Even Dexter, who finished with 207 runs, was overshadowed.

A few days later, the new one-day champions entertained the West Indies in front of another 15,000 full-house at Hove

– and beat them, Jim contributing 39 as Sussex won by four wickets with three overs to spare in a 55-overs contest chasing a target of 178. Griffith was not included in the tourists' line-up. It was the penultimate game of a 38-match tour which had started back in April at Eastbourne against Colonel LC Stevens' XI.

With Jim and Dexter regularly on England duty during the mid-1960s Sussex lacked the strength in depth to mount a sustained challenge for the Championship but, buoyed by their success in 1963, they grew stronger as a one-day force. A year after their first Lord's triumph they were back there again in the Gillette Cup final, this time against Warwickshire.

"Ted got there late and only just arrived in time for the toss. I was going to go out with their captain MJK Smith when Ted turned up and tossed up in his civvies," remembers Jim. "The dew was glistening off the pitch and we knew with the 10.30am start that the ball would swing. MJK decided to bat first. The first ball from Ian Thomson to Norman Horner swung so much it was nearly called a wide."

Thomson's new-ball spell brought him 3-14 and he finished with overall figures of 4-23. Smith, who was to lead England in South Africa the following winter, chose the Sussex seamer for the tour party on the strength of his performance that day. Warwickshire were dismissed for 127 and when Sussex replied the haze had lifted and batting was a lot easier in late summer sunshine.

"All the crowd wanted was to see Ted bat for a bit," said Jim. "But they had little chance. When we came together we were 97-2 and only needed another 31." Sussex retained their trophy with ease.

It was another 39 years before Sussex won the County Championship for the first time and Jim was as proud as anyone when Murray Goodwin hit the winning runs against Leicestershire at Hove in 2003.

By then one-day cricket in England had become unrecognisable from the somewhat rudimentary game played by those pioneers back in 1963. Six years after the Gillette Cup the concept of the Rothmans Cavaliers was effectively standardised with the advent of the 40-over John Player League with limited run-ups and eight overs maximum per bowler – perfect for the Sunday afternoon audience at the ground or on BBC2.

A generation learned to love the game through watching those broadcasts where Peter Walker or Peter West would do some links five minutes before the camera – only one behind the arm remember – would pick out John Arlott and Jim Laker, usually perched precariously on a flimsy wooden gantry at places like Glastonbury, Bradford and Ilford, for commentary.

"It was great fun and the crowds loved it," said Jim. "For starters, the ground was the only place in England you could get a drink after 2pm on a Sunday afternoon."

By 2003 counties were playing 20-over bun-fights in front of full houses.

"I think that side of 1963 would have been pretty good at Twenty20," reflects Jim. "It certainly suited me and you would have had a job to set a field to someone like Ted. He was a magnificent batsman because he hit it straight. You can't put a

fielder in front of the sight-screen can you?"

MUSHTAQ AHMED

2006: An Enduring Legacy

FOUR YEARS AFTER he played his last game for Sussex, Mushtaq Ahmed's legacy is still evident on every day of cricket that is played at Hove.

During the intervals schoolchildren bound on to the outfield, get out their plastic bats and enjoy their own games. But it's not the fast men they are trying to emulate as they run in to bowl to their mates or fathers. Instead, the ball is gripped tightly in small hands and they bound in off a few paces to bowl rudimentary leg-spin.

Anyone who watched or even spent time with Mushtaq during six sensational seasons with Sussex, when his quixotic mixture of googlies, leg-breaks, flippers and top-spinners propelled the county to the top of English cricket, was instantly charmed. He would often sit on the players' balcony at Hove during the break, dragging on a cigarette, feet up on the rail watching the youngsters trying to emulate their new hero. And if time allowed he would stroll across the outfield and offer a word of gentle advice to anyone who caught his eye.

Perhaps this is Mushy's greatest legacy: that he inspired a generation of Sussex youngsters to take up leg-spin. And if one day one of them would admire from the balcony plays for the county and even helps them to bring more success to Hove he will be as fulfilled as he was after any of those many matches he helped Sussex to win.

"He used to find it quite amusing that all these kids on the outfield at Hove would be trying to bowl leg spin," remembers Chris Adams, his captain throughout those six seasons. "But I think secretly he was quite proud of that. And when the kids used to queue up to get his autograph he would quite often remember them from watching during the interval and give them a word of encouragement which, of course, meant the world to them."

The youngsters would even practise Mushy's appeal during those games, turning to Dad or an imaginary umpire, arms raised in expectation. Mushy's persistent appealing would upset opposition batsmen. Some called it excessive but they rarely had an answer when asked which bowler hit the pads more often than Mushtaq.

In his first season with Sussex in 2003 he took 103 wickets. Not bad for a bowler whom most of the Sussex committee considered well past his best when the coach Peter Moores asked them at the end of the previous year to sanction his signing. After some gentle persuasion Moores got his way. Leg-spin was the most difficult of the game's arts to master and usually the easiest to lose. Full tosses and long hops, kicking the turf in frustration, they can be a captain's worst nightmare and even Adams admits he had his reservations when Mushtaq, who had been playing for Little Stoke in the Staffordshire League on a £12,500 contract, arrived towards the end of the 2002 season, battered old-fashioned cricket coffin in tow, to talk terms.

A year later he was being feted throughout Sussex after making the biggest contribution to the first Championship in Sussex's history. Bearded, bouncing, smiling Mushtaq, who left Somerset under a cloud in 1998 and whose international career was considered a thing of the past, had kick-started the most successful period in Sussex's long and hitherto often inglorious history. But if 2003 was Mushy's year then how do you quantify his contribution in 2006?

By then, his fourth season back in county cricket, most batsmen worth their salt should have been able to work out a game-plan against him yet he finished with 102 wickets, one fewer than 2003, and another Championship medal as well after taking 26 wickets in his last two games.

That haul came from 15 matches, as opposed to 16 four years earlier, after he was forced to miss the mid-summer game with Kent because of injury. Those wickets came at an average of 19.91 each and included 11 five-wicket innings and four ten-wicket match hauls, the most celebrated, of course, the final one at Trent Bridge where he produced a superlative display in Nottinghamshire's second innings with 9-48 off 11.3 overs.

When he bowled Ryan Sidebottom to claim his 100th wicket his reaction provided one of the unforgettable memories during Sussex's second golden age as he sank to the turf to offer a silent prayer while his respectful team-mates held back their celebrations for a few seconds before engulfing him in hugs.

I interviewed Mushy many times during his six years at Hove and getting this modest man to talk about his own achievements was as fiendishly difficult as trying to pick his googly. Even now, six years after that day at Trent Bridge when he produced the best bowling performance of his career, he does not regard what he achieved that day as anything remarkable on a personal level. For him, the pride is what his performance gave to others: his team-mates and the 300 or so Sussex supporters who were there to witness that second Championship. "That's where the real enjoyment lies," he says quietly.

Even now, when he reflects on a career which ended in 2008 after persistent knee trouble forced him to retire and concentrate on coaching, he finds it hard to compare and contrast those great years with Sussex.

He says: "I remember trying to get a contract with an English county in 2002 but nobody wanted me, perhaps because my time with Somerset ended badly. Fortunately, Sussex did want me. I know Peter Moores had to persuade the club to sign me but I knew once I had joined Sussex that I would be happy there. And if I was happy, I also knew I would bowl well for them."

· Mushtaq took 103 wickets in his first season to become the first bowler to take 100 wickets since Andy Caddick and Courtney Walsh in 1998. Famously, he arrived for the final game of the season, when Sussex needed six points against Leicestershire to claim the title, without his whites. "I was so nervous," he laughed. So were Sussex supporters, the Holy Grail within tantalising reach. They need not have worried.

The wear and tear of a long season – he bowled 836.3 overs in the Championship alone – meant he was unable to bowl in the second innings because of a groin problem but four wickets on the first day, including Brad Hodge as his 100th victim of the season, helped lay the foundation for Murray Goodwin and Jason Lewry to lead Sussex to glory. "It is a long time since we won that Championship but there aren't many days when I don't think about that season," he says. "God had put me in a dark place to test me in 2003. But I waited for the sunrise and it came."

Two seasons, 162 wickets and 1,351 Championship overs later Mushy was 36 and there was more than a hint of grey in that bushy beard of his. When he returned to Hove in April 2006 he admitted that he had his eyes on playing until he was 40. It was inevitable that when he retired he would turn to coaching although things certainly did not pan out in the way he thought they would then. He had already resisted one overture from Pakistan to join their coaching set-up but by the end of the season Bob Woolmer had persuaded him to become his assistant.

At the start of 2006 he had made a conscious effort to try and take more wickets during the early weeks of the campaign. He hated the cold weather and in early-season days gripping the ball was often a challenge. When he wasn't bowling he would be swathed in sweaters, his fingers clinging to hand-warmers, or sitting by the heater in the dressing room, venturing out only occasionally to check the score or puff away on a cigarette.

He says: "I loved being back at Hove, seeing my team-mates and the familiar faces around the club. But I preferred England when it was a bit warmer. There was no reason why I couldn't take more wickets despite the cold though. I talked to (coach) Mark Robinson and (captain) Chris Adams about it. It was a case of being mentally stronger I suppose."

The sun shone throughout the season-opener against Warwickshire at Hove but a slow pitch was not made for bowlers, seam or spin. In total, 1,168 runs were scored and Mushtaq toiled away for 43 overs in Warwickshire's only innings for the wickets of Jim Troughton and number ten Neil Carter.

A week later Sussex travelled to the Rose Bowl to face Hampshire. Perhaps it was the arrival of compatriot Rana Naved that, despite the cold and a damp pitch seemingly made for seam and not spin, he took seven wickets in Hampshire's second innings as Sussex won their first game of the season with a day to spare. Five of his victims were given out lbw by former Hampshire player Trevor Jesty.

The momentum was maintained a week later against Yorkshire at Headingley although it was Rana rather than Mushtaq who was the stand-out overseas performer as he took 11 wickets against the county who had turned him down while he was playing in the Bradford League. Matt Prior's hundred helped ease Sussex to a five-wicket win yet amazingly, after two wins and a draw in their first three games, the county were only third in the table. "We always expected a challenge from Lancashire in those days," remembered Mushy. "But there were a lot of strong counties that season and we had to work very hard for every game we won."

Champions Nottinghamshire arrived at Hove in early May and Mushtaq was involved in the most controversial incident of his Sussex career. On his way to six first-innings wickets, Mushtaq dismissed Chris Read lbw for a duck. Read, furious at Mushtaq's perpetual appealing, confronted him on the boundary edge in front of bemused spectators before he was led back up the steps to the dressing room by team-mate

David Hussey. The pair later shook hands after the umpires decided not to take the matter further and Mushtaq dismissed it as a heat of the moment incident.

He says: "I had a lot of respect for my opponents and Chris was and still is a fine player. His reaction surprised me but it was out of character. Looking back, I think the fielders around the bat irritated him. About five minutes after I got him out fifth ball he came down the steps and started to argue with me. I told him I didn't want to make an issue out of it but if he had an issue with me I was sorry. When we met in the umpires' room later I told him that I considered him a friend. We shook hands and it was soon forgotten."

What was not forgotten in a hurry was a remarkable Sussex fightback. Chasing 161 to win, Nottinghamshire were 40-1 when Rana and Lewry began swinging and reversing the Dukes ball. They took seven wickets between them in 23 overs, Mushtaq mopped up the rest and Sussex won by 41 runs to go to the top of the table for the first time.

Perhaps the game where Sussex realised that they would again be challenging for the title was at Durham, a venue which had always been good to them, in late May, although a grassy pitch seemed especially prepared for a rare appearance by the hosts' Steve Harmison and to negate Mushtaq.

Mushtaq finished with match figures of 10-37 from 20 overs after taking five wickets in both innings and Sussex won inside two days by an innings despite only scoring 229. Durham lost all ten second-innings wickets in an hour for just 33 runs.

Four wins out of five became five out of six at Horsham in early June. It was a ground Mushtaq always enjoyed. Occasionally he would be collared – the tennis courts at

Town End were a temptation most batsmen could not ignore when Mushy came into the attack – but the wicket invariably turned by day three and it offered the spinners bounce as well. He says: "I liked Horsham. The cricket there was always good for the spectators because there was always plenty happening. Batsmen scored quickly, the boundaries were not big but it also offered bowlers something. Some of my best games for Sussex were there."

The 2006 festival fixture continued along similar lines to so many there during the Mushtaq era. Sussex made 376 after winning the toss and then Mushtaq got amongst the opposition – in this case Middlesex, although not until Owais Shah had mastered him with a brilliant 126 despite suffering from cramp because he tended to grip the bat-handle too hard.

According to Mushtaq, it was probably the best innings he had seen played against him by a county batsman. Former Yorkshire and Australia left-hander Darren Lehmann was another opponent who occasionally mastered Mushy. "But remember, it only takes one good ball to get someone out!" was, invariably, his response. Sussex built on a lead of 110 and eventually set Middlesex 481. Just before lunch on the fourth day they had won by 224 runs.

There were another five wickets for him in the next game at Liverpool, but apart from that and Jason Lewry's 500th first-class wicket there wasn't much for Sussex to celebrate after a two-day defeat to Lancashire. They went into the Twenty20 break with a five-point lead over Hampshire and a contented leg-spinner happy that, for a few weeks at least, his workload would not be quite as arduous.

"I was determined to take more wickets in the early months but it was perhaps better than I could have hoped for," said

Mushtaq. "I wanted to take 30 wickets by the time we started Twenty20 and I had reached 46. Things were going well for the team at that stage and Mark Robinson was settling in well as the coach. He had different ideas to Peter Moores but like Moores he believed in the team ethic and that was important for us."

When Championship cricket resumed five weeks later there was no Mushtaq. For the first time since 2003 he missed a four-day game because of a persistent neck problem.

The game against Kent was drawn. In his absence off-spinner Ollie Rayner and Mike Yardy bowled 54 overs of spin on a desperately slow pitch and Rayner picked up three wickets but Kent held on for a draw with seven wickets down.

Mushtaq returned against Middlesex at Southgate a few days later in stifling heat. A dry pitch, on a ground which traditionally favoured spin, appeared to be tailor-made for Mushtaq, but the injury was clearly troubling him. He bowled 42 wicket-less overs in Middlesex's first innings and although he and Rayner shared five wickets in the second dig Sussex were ultimately frustrated by the loss of 24 overs on the final day to rain after the long, hot spell finally broke with a spectacular thunderstorm. Nevertheless, with Lancashire losing to Kent, Sussex still led the table by 13 points, although the positions were to be reversed a few days later.

Sussex had not won at Edgbaston in a Championship game since Imran Khan bowled them to victory in 1982 and only once since 1961 yet Mushtaq enjoyed bowling in Brum. "I had success there," he says. "There was always some help for the spinners and I liked Birmingham. I always met up with friends during that game. But in all my time with Sussex we never won a Championship match there, although a few times we ought to have."

This was one. Sussex lost all ten first-innings wickets in a session to concede a deficit of 129 runs but Mushtaq bowled Sussex into contention on the third day with 5-39 in 18.3 overs. Sussex had five sessions to score 270 and were in a strong position at 178-3 but a pitch which deteriorated badly was no friend to batsmen and they were dismissed for 256. Close, but not close enough. Lancashire now led the table by a point.

At least Sussex's star turn was in good health. Mushtaq had taken his tally to 62 wickets with six more in Birmingham and for his county there was further succour when the touring Pakistanis declined to select him for the second Test. Speculation that they might turn to Mushtaq, three years after his last Test appearance, had been intensifying but in the end his close friend Inzamam-ul-Haq persisted instead with another leg-spinner, Danish Kaneria. Sussex breathed a sigh of relief.

Next up came a meeting of the top two and one of the most compelling of all the Championship contests during Sussex's title-winning years against Lancashire. There were queues to get in on the first day and after Sussex had made 439 on a dry pitch Mushtaq was soon in action.

This time, though, he found his match. Stuart Law, who had a spectacular record against Sussex over the years, eased to a hundred and there was the rare sight of a young batsman emboldened rather than embarrassed when he came face to face with Mushtaq. Gareth Cross hit 26 off one over and Mushtaq was unable to complete his 19th over, disappearing into the pavilion for treatment to a groin problem.

Sussex set Lancashire 392 to win on the final day when Mushtaq did bowl, albeit in some discomfort. "It was one of the bravest things I ever saw in my years at Sussex," remembers Chris Adams. "Mushy wasn't even 50% fit but he knew how important it was for him to be out there trying to put their batsmen under pressure. We had enough runs to be sure of not losing but our seamers would not have bowled Lancashire out on that pitch which was still flat and still slow on the fourth day."

Mushtaq finally got his first wicket when Glen Chapple was sixth out after tea and it seemed to inspire him. He took two more wickets including Dominic Cork who was ninth out with eight balls of the game remaining. Number three Mal Loye and last man Gary Keedy survived, Loye finishing undefeated on 148. His joy when the last delivery had been negotiated was unconfined, although Sussex had at least regained the lead albeit by a single point.

With no Championship cricket for another 11 days Mushtaq was allowed to return to Lahore to rest his aching limbs. His return coincided with the birth, a few days ahead of schedule, of his fourth child and when he returned to Hove in mid-August for the game against Durham at Hove he looked rejuvenated. "That was an important period in the season for me," he says. "I had some time at home and to be there when our daughter was born was a wonderful blessing. It helped me forget about the aches and pains to be honest."

Sussex had four games to go and fortunately for Mushtaq their next opponents were Durham, who had a terrible record against him and also at Hove. Mushtaq took 8-121 in the match as Sussex completed an innings win just after lunch on the third day. They were now level on points with

Lancashire at the top, with Hampshire a distant third 22 points behind.

Shane Warne brought Hampshire to Hove at the end of August knowing they had to win to keep their slim challenge alive. In the event the weather won. Rain and bad light affected the last three days with 91 overs lost and the game ended in a draw. Mushtaq took three first-innings wickets (Warne collected six) but only bowled 12 overs in the second, as Adams tried to manage the workload of his weary players with two games to go – both away from home – with his side eight points clear.

By the time they arrived at Canterbury for their penultimate fixture, Sussex were running on empty. "A county season is a grind and when you are challenging for the title the mental pressure is as hard to deal with as the physical effort required," says Adams. "But we were fortunate that season that we were allowed to give Mushy a bit of time off when we did. He came back refreshed and although he wasn't totally fit all season really he was as good as he'd been for a while."

Kent were another county whose batsmen had always struggled to combat Mushtaq. There was some turn, but not excessive, yet in the first innings he took 6-58 including top scorer Martin van Jaarsveld for 116. Sussex didn't fare a lot better when they batted and it needed an unbeaten 25 from Mushtaq at the end to help earn his side a first-innings lead of 48.

Mushtaq always took his batting seriously although towards the end of his career he did not fancy the fast stuff. But he had a good eye and he hit bowlers in areas where they were infrequently deposited. "He was unorthodox," says Adams. "He improvised quite a bit and he was quite strong. When he hit the ball it stayed hit, but we never expected him to last long against genuinely quick bowling. Then it was a case of self-preservation, which you could totally understand. The last thing we wanted was for him to break a finger or something."

On the second day 16 wickets fell. Kent resumed on day three with a lead of 138 and their last two wickets added 22 precious runs when Adams used Jason Lewry and Yasir Arafat rather than Mushtaq at the start of play. Within three balls of his introduction he had claimed his 13th wicket of the game, finishing with 7-74 in the second innings and 13-132 in the match, his best figures for Sussex. Matt Prior picked up four stumpings. In seven games against Kent since 2003, Mushtaq had taken 52 wickets.

Sussex's target of 161 looked straightforward but nerves got the better of their batsmen. Adams and Prior put on 31 for the fifth wicket but when off-spinner James Tredwell took two wickets in the same over after lunch Sussex were 145-8, still 16 runs short of victory. James Kirtley came out to join Mushtaq. For their team-mates the tension was palpable. Prior took himself off for a solitary lap of the ground. Adams ordered the rest of his team to stay where they were, in either the dressing room or on the balcony, frightened that if they moved a wicket would fall. An ashen-faced Mark Robinson could only stare out to the middle from his perch on the balcony.

Kirtley did not have too many shots in his locker but he could get into line and didn't give his wicket away. "He was the ideal partner in that situation" says Mushtaq. "The field was quite attacking and the pressure wasn't really on us because the bowlers knew that if they bowled a poor ball we could put it away." Slowly the target was whittled down and the hundred or so Sussex supporters exhaled a collective sigh of relief when Mushtaq pulled a ball from James Tredwell between two fielders on the mid-wicket boundary for a precious four. A few minutes later, as they crowded in front of the away dressing room, Mushtaq emerged onto the balcony wondering what all the fuss was about.

"When you look at the last two games that season the Kent game was crucial for us," says Mushtaq. "It meant whatever Lancashire did from their game in hand against Durham we would go to Trent Bridge for the last match in a very strong position. To be honest I always thought James Kirtley and I would get those runs. I was quite relaxed and when you are not tense you can play your normal game."

There was a long build-up to the denouement at Trent Bridge and not a particularly happy one. Three days before, Sussex had played Nottinghamshire in the 40-over competition knowing that victory would secure the title if Essex lost, but they batted nervously and the chief beneficiary was the previously unheralded home seamer Gareth Clough whose mixture of gentle away swingers and in-duckers brought him 6-25, easily the best one-day figures of his career. Nottinghamshire won by eight wickets with more than ten overs to spare and Sussex finished third as the title went to Essex, even though they were beaten by Durham.

Before the Championship game Sussex won an important stand-off with the ECB, who were keen to rest Michael Yardy ahead of the Champions Trophy in India. Sussex said no and picked him as well as bringing back Rana Naved, who had finished his touring commitments with Pakistan, in place of Yasir Arafat.

Lancashire's game in hand against Durham had been drawn so, with an eight-point lead, Sussex needed 14 points to guarantee the title. Lancashire were at third-placed Hampshire while of interest to Nottinghamshire was the game between Yorkshire and Durham, who were nine points behind and involved, it seemed, in a battle to avoid joining Middlesex in relegation. Notts needed just three points to make sure of survival but Graeme Swann was absent with an elbow problem and Mark Ealham was playing as a batsman because of a rib problem.

Adams won the toss and Sussex batted but made a nervous start. Carl Hopkinson was run out by a direct hit from Samit Patel at extra cover before a brief hiatus because of bad light. When they resumed Yardy and Richard Montgomerie took Sussex to 94-1 at lunch as a hot sun burnt off the early dampness and the pitch eased.

Shortly after the interval Sussex got a break. Yardy was dropped in the slips by Stephen Fleming who had to have four stitches inserted in the little finger of his left hand, an injury which would inhibit his batting. Yardy and Montgomerie put on 144 before Montgomerie edged to slip but Yardy pressed on to his third century of the season before falling for 119. Murray Goodwin, having helped Yardy add 110, then put on 122 with Adams who made 72 off 91 balls. Prior kept up the attack, hitting his first six scoring shots to the boundary as the plunder of an anodyne attack, badly missing Swann, continued.

Sussex reached their first target – 400 and five batting bonus points – but Goodwin was denied a century when Charlie Shreck bowled him for 99 in the last over of the day. Sussex closed day one on 420-5 and Mushtaq, feet up on the pavilion balcony, noted that left-arm spinner Patel was getting a bit of turn already. "We couldn't have had a better day," reflected Adams afterwards. "Apart from Murray missing his century it went as well as we could have hoped."

Although the second day dawned sunny and warm, Adams was wary of a poorer weather forecast for later in the game. He only wanted to bat once and the instructions to Prior and Robin Martin-Jenkins when they resumed the innings was to accelerate. Once again they were aided by some poor Nottinghamshire bowling and even sloppier fielding. Both raced to rapid fifties before Martin-Jenkins was badly dropped by wicketkeeper David Alleyne. The significance of that reprieve would only become truly apparent the following day.

Sussex added 140 in 27.2 overs without losing a wicket as Prior and Martin-Jenkins posted the fourth century stand of the innings. It was the first time six Sussex batsmen had scored half-centuries in the same innings since 1904. Adams, with 72, was the second-lowest scorer. When he declared 35 minutes before lunch on 560-5 it meant Nottinghamshire had only collected one of the three points they needed to make sure of their First Division place.

A total of 250 would secure two batting points and safety and when they progressed to 58-1 during the afternoon and then 142-3 they were on course. Mushtaq had picked up the second wicket after Alleyne, like so many county batsmen encountering him for the first time, played back to a googly but David Hussey began to counter-attack with Patel. Then, just before tea, things started to happen.

Martin-Jenkins found some extra bounce and Patel drove to extra cover then Ealham played back to Mushtaq and was bowled. Moments later came the key wicket as Fleming, batting down at number seven because of his finger injury, swept Mushtaq and got a top-edge which Adams snaffled. Hussey then edged Martin-Jenkins and Montgomerie at slip took a sharp catch. Nottinghamshire had lost four wickets in 13 balls and were now 144-7. One batting point, never mind two, looked unlikely.

Paul Franks was dropped after tea but Sussex were in the ascendancy. Adams brought back Rana to give Mushtaq a breather and he and Lewry took a wicket each before Mushtaq returned to wrap things up with his fourth wicket when Franks edged to slip. From 143-3 Nottinghamshire wickets had scattered like leaves on the breeze and they were all out for 165. Their only consolation was the news from Headingley where Durham, needing 400 to secure enough batting points to overtake them, were 203-6.

Trailing by 395, Notts went in again with 18 overs of the day remaining. Adams had to turn to Mushtaq and Yardy to bowl spin after five overs with the umpires threatening to take the players off because of fading light. "My hand was forced to some extent but it was only a matter of time before Mushy would have been on anyway," says Adams. "Sometimes you felt the seamers were only there to rough the ball up a bit so he could grip it better! He'd bowled 20 overs in the first innings which by Mushy's standards wasn't masses and he felt fine. We also knew the forecast for Friday wasn't great so if we could make inroads that evening we would buy ourselves a bit of time if it did rain."

The impact was instant. On 32, Will Smith became Mushtaq's first victim of the innings when he missed a googly and was leg before. Carl Hopkinson, an outstanding close-to-the-bat fielder, caught Alleyne with only four more runs added then Fleming, still struggling with his sore finger, edged to

Adams after a couple of blows over the top off Kirtley. Notts were 45-3 and added three before Darren Bicknell fell to the Mushtaq-Hopkinson combination in what was the final innings of his career.

Being dismissed by such a fine bowler was no disgrace but Bicknell's reaction did him little credit. Convinced his bat had made no contact with the ball (TV replays backed up his claim), he stood his ground for several seconds before stomping off. It was only when he neared the pavilion that he stood to salute the standing ovation from all sides of Trent Bridge.

After 11 overs, and even with spin at both ends, the light was too bad. Nottinghamshire were 50-4, still 345 behind and back in Sussex supporters were making plans to head up the M1 the following morning.

Seven wickets, including four in three overs in the second innings, was, of course, all in a day's work for Mushtaq. "We'd had a good day," he said with typical understatement. "The key for us was getting those quick wickets after lunch. The pitch was pretty good to bat on and of course we caught well, especially around the bat. We could maintain attacking fields with so many runs to play with."

The following morning dawned, as the forecasters had predicted, overcast. Rain was due around 1pm and the likelihood was it would last for most of the afternoon. There were even a few spots in the air when Adams led his team down the pavilion steps just after 11am. What did surprise the skipper was the number of familiar faces he could see as he walked onto the outfield. Around 300 Sussex supporters had arrived in the expectation of a celebration and with the Nottinghamshire public having given up on their side they made up the majority of the crowd dotted around that most handsome of grounds.

Nottinghamshire's approach soon became evident. Doomed to certain defeat they opted for a counter-attack as Patel crashed Kirtley through the on-side for four, but they were futile blows. In his third over Mushtaq made the breakthrough when Hussey was completely flummoxed by what had become almost his stock ball – the googly – and bowled for ten. "Ninety-eight!" was the cry from the stattos behind the arm. Mushtaq needed two more wickets to reach 100. He didn't have to wait long. Patel, summing up the spinelessness of his side's batting, swung horribly across the line and a few minutes later Ryan Sidebottom did exactly the same. Mushtaq fell to his knees, kissed the turf and offered a silent prayer to Allah.

Mushtaq wrapped the innings up with the wickets of Ealham and Harris. He would have had all ten had Kirtley not picked up Paul Franks. "If it had been allowed I'm sure Mushy would have bowled at both ends!" said Kirtley a few hours later as Sussex began their celebrations. His figures of 9-48 were the best of his career and the best at Trent Bridge since Essex all-rounder Morris Nichols took 9-32 in 1936.

For the second successive game Mushtaq finished with 13 wickets in the match and Sussex had won convincingly by an innings and 245 runs. Durham, meanwhile, were cruising past 400 and Nottinghamshire were heading for relegation the year after winning the title.

By the time the silverware arrived – the ECB had clearly not anticipated Sussex would wrap things up so quickly – it was raining steadily. Mushtaq had been chaired off the pitch by compatriots Rana Naved and Yasir Arafat, who had played an important part in the season's successes before Adams lifted the modest trophy for the second time in four years.

Following any victory it was those precious moments in the dressing room afterwards that Mushtaq enjoyed the most. A hoary rendition of Sussex by the Sea – although even by 2006 Mushtaq admitted he wasn't quite sure of the words – and the company of friends was what he enjoyed. Their work-rate and strong team ethic had helped turn a good team into a very good team. That and the input of star turns like Mushtaq.

When he faced the media there were few revelations, as was often the case with Mushtaq. "I would like to thank Allah for giving us victory and for winning the toss," he said, to no-one's great surprise. "I would also like to thank Allah for he has clearly played his part," added his captain sitting alongside him. The journalists started to laugh but Adams was being serious. "He has brought his religion to the club and the players we have understand and respect his beliefs. It is a big part of what has made us so successful."

Six years later Mushtaq remains heavily involved in English cricket. The creaking knees finally gave way in 2008 and he retired from playing but it wasn't long before Peter Moores, whose foresight back in 2003 had revived his career, found him a place on his support staff after his appointment as England's coach.

It was a source of much regret to Mushtaq when Moores lost his job but his replacement Andy Flower retained Mushtaq and he played a key role working with Graeme Swann and Monty Panesar as England became the number one-ranked Test nation. When he took a break from England commitments in the summer of 2012 Adams, by then in charge of Surrey cricket, hired him for a month as a consultant.

When he retired Mushtaq had taken 476 Championship wickets for Sussex and helped the county win three titles and three one-day trophies. "In all my time at Sussex what I appreciated most from everyone – coaches, team-mates, supporters – was that they always tried to maintain a positive attitude," he reflected. "That was difficult sometimes because we did have days and seasons, such as 2004, when things didn't go our way. It definitely helped me. People always looked for the good things and that inspired me, particularly on days when I was feeling tired or suffering from pain.

"We won three Championships but comparing them, even now, is difficult. When I arrived in 2003 there was no expectation but by the end of the season there was pressure. That's when my faith became even more important.

"I always believed I could deliver strong performances and when I got 13 wickets against Kent in the game at the end of 2006 I really did believe I could do it again against Nottinghamshire. I knew everyone was behind me and mentally I felt so strong. When I switched off, which sometimes happened, I bowled bad balls.

"But that week I felt so calm and focused on what we had to do. It was a wonderful time – all of it. There isn't a day even now when I don't think back to my six seasons with Sussex. I would not have changed a single moment of it."

Hawkins & Co
Brighton

Cox

Copyright

1926: The Guv'nor's Game

TWO THINGS HAVE been synonymous with Sussex cricket in the last 170 years – the great tradition of family cricketers playing for Sussex and the county's out-grounds.

The story of the great cricketing families of Sussex, the Langridges, Parkses and Coxes in the years either side of the Second World War and, more recently, the Lenhams and Wells have been extensively chronicled over the decades and Sussex's history would be a lot more prosaic without their own generation games.

The tradition of out-ground cricket in Sussex is just as quixotic. These days Arundel and Horsham offer supporters the opportunity to watch their team in quintessential English surroundings and while the loss of county cricket in East Sussex is a matter of regret there is the hope that one day Sussex might return to Eastbourne or Hastings.

Worthing and Chichester, sadly, went a long time ago and there is always a concern that another of the established festivals might disappear or that cricket at Arundel and Horsham will happen on a rota basis.

That would be a shame for Sussex are one of the few remaining counties to take cricket to two out-grounds every year. "We are Sussex CCC, not Brighton & Hove," insists former chief executive Dave Brooks, a firm fan of festival cricket.

The Arundel Festival is relatively new. The first Championship game there was staged in 1990 but Horsham, apart from a 26-year hiatus between 1956 and 1983, has staged a county week since 1908 including non-first class fixtures in 1971, 1974 and 1979.

There have been many improvements to the ground in the intervening 104 years yet in many ways it remains unspoiled and largely unchanged over the last century with the wooded slopes of Denne Hill beyond the railway line at one end and the spire of St Mary's Church dominating the skyline at the town end. The best way of entering the ground is not down the narrow Cricketfield Road but, as it would have been back at the start of the last century, down The Causeway, through the church yard, across the wooden bridge and up the slight incline past what was Joker Oakes's cottage.

What were we saying about Sussex's family tradition? None is more strongly associated with Horsham than Alfred "Joker" Oakes and his sons Charles and Jack, both of whom played for the county. Joker did not wear the six martlets, although he was a fine club player for Horsham and a former captain of the town's football club. Instead, he became a groundsman while still in his teens and took over duties at Horsham in 1911, continuing in the job for another 44 years before retiring in 1954, two years before Sussex staged its last festival week there and did not return for nearly three decades.

During Cricket Week the entire Oakes family mucked in. Jack, who died in 1997, recalled having to take the week off school to help. His sisters, May and Dorothy, would clean the players' pads and boots. Former club president Dr John Dew, as synonymous with Horsham as anyone in the club's history, recalled Joker as "someone who mellowed in old age". He continued: "When he retired he loved sitting on the boundary edge during the festival chewing over things with his old cronies. He did used to like a grumble, which is where he got the nickname from I suppose. But he knew how to prepare a wicket."

Charles, who died in 2007, arguably lost his best cricketing years to the Second World War. But he scored more than 10,000 runs and took 449 wickets for the county, once memorably hitting a six into his father's back garden when he took a hundred off a strong Surrey attack.

Like Charles, Jack was also born in his father's cottage. Statistics suggest his career was less successful than his elder brother's but he was nevertheless a useful middle-order hitter who played 128 times for the county. His finest hour came in 1947 when he picked up 7-64 against Warwickshire with his off breaks. In 1950 he scored 151 against Cambridge University.

"We had a pretty tough upbringing," Charles remembered. "My mother used to stop me at the door and ask how I'd gotten on and if I hadn't done very well my father wasn't pleased. Jack hit the ball harder than me, though I don't think he did himself justice really. He didn't get the runs he should have."

For the Oakes family, Horsham was their very own backyard. The other Sussex family with close connections to Horsham was the Coxes and similarities between Joker Oakes and George Cox senior cannot be ignored. Sussex historian John Marshall described Cox as a "nuggety old warhorse with splashes of grey in his military moustache and a tongue that belied a pair of kindly eyes". Like Joker, George Rubens Cox was something of a curmudgeon who doled out praise, even to his own children, reluctantly.

George junior carried on the family tradition either side of the Second World War and played for the county for nearly 30 years, but even his finest achievements failed to stir much of a sense of familial pride. In July 1939 young George took 232 off the Northamptonshire attack at Kettering and the next day made 182 at Hove against Lancashire. He returned to the family home in Warnham, a few miles from Horsham, that evening no doubt feeling rather pleased with himself. "What's the matter with you then, gone mad or something," growled his father from his armchair beside the hearth. Pleasantries did not come as easy to Old George as playing the game.

Cricket has been played at Warnham for more than 200 years while the village's most famous father and son served Sussex for 64 years. Old George made his debut in 1895 and was still playing for the county aged 54, just two years after he enjoyed the finest moment of his career at Horsham and one of the best individual performances in the county's history when he took 17 wickets against Warwickshire in June 1926.

These days, any cricketer still playing at the top level into his 40s is regarded as some sort of phenomenon. George Cox routed Warwickshire aged 52. His economical bowling action – left-arm slows mixed with top-spinners – helped prolong his longevity – but so did his fastidious and seemingly relentless attention to physical fitness.

Arthur Gilligan captained him regularly during the 1920s. "When he was about to come into bowl he would rub his hand on the ground and then measure out his run," remembered Gilligan. "Then he would stand and glare at the batsman, rub his hand across his mouth before running up to the wicket.

"Over and over he would send down, concealing his heavily disguised slower ball and the fast swinger which would get him many victims."

Sports scientists and fitness trainers were a long way off back in 1926 and, even if they were around, it's likely that Old George would have relied on his own methods to maintain that boxer's build of his when a lot of his speed off the pitch was generated by a powerful pair of shoulders.

Back then most players – pros and amateurs – had scant if any regard for physical training, relying instead on playing the game itself to build up fitness and stamina. His methods were simple: plenty of walking – he thought nothing of strolling for ten miles on a daily basis around Horsham and the surrounding villages – while a crude but perfectly workable Turkish bath at home would help sweat away any excess pounds.

As recently as 1924 – his 50th year – Old George had taken 42 wickets and although by 1926 his appearances had become more sporadic Gilligan would call on him when he was without Maurice Tate, who by then was an established England bowler.

Before heading back to his home ground, Cox had played just three Championship games in 1926 and taken two wickets so he hardly arrived at the ground in great form. In the county's previous game – a low-scoring affair at the Wagon Works Ground in Gloucester – Gilligan and Tate had shared ten wickets between them as Gloucestershire were routed for just 58 in their first innings while Cox bowled five wicket-less overs in the second as Sussex completed only their second win of the season, the other having come at the Oval.

The following day, Saturday 5th June, was bright and sunny in contrast to much of the previous week when regular downpours had saturated Joker's county wicket – then left uncovered of course – and hampered preparations for his biggest week of the year, even though he had use of a motorised mower for the first time.

"The ground was still full of moisture from the soaking it had taken during the week and a heavy dew the previous night added to its slowness during a cloudy morning," reported the *Sussex Daily News*.

More than eight decades later Cricket Week is still an important part of Horsham's town calendar but back then it was arguably the highlight of the year for the town's folk. Shops and streets would be decorated with bunting and the organisers put on a show after each day's play which would always be attended by players from both sides.

In 1926 the entertainment committee "proudly presented that highly amusing farce in three acts by Sidney Blow and Douglas Hoare, *Lord Richard in the Pantry*". Later in the week there would be a well-attended Carnival Ball (fancy dress optional).

A crowd of around 2,000 paid a shilling each (sixpence after 4pm) to watch the first day, among them EV Lucas, one of the pre-eminent literary figures of the period and a great cricket lover. To him Horsham looked its very best. "The primitiveness of the pavilion and discomfort of much of the seating appear to fit in appropriately," he wrote. "It's all preposterous but ever so picturesque, like the haunt of some cricketing Pierrots."

Reading the *Sussex Daily News* reports 86 years later, as Cox himself might have done when puffing on his pipe at his fireside, it is evident just how important the social aspect of the festival was. It wasn't until after five windy paragraphs, when everything was chronicled in detail except the cricket itself, that Cox's feat in the first innings, when he took eight wickets, even got a cursory mention.

Readers were first treated to two lengthy discourses on "The Tea Hostesses" and "In The Enclosure" which described in great deal what the ladies were wearing and even how they had arrived at the ground. Some might have been flattered by the description of their attire, others less so. While "Mr Tremewen brought pretty Miss Marjorie Tremewen, who was very attractive in a subdued shade of apricot, Lady Graham wore a black gown with dull red hat."

Warwickshire batted first with their formidable captain RES "Bob" Wyatt and John Parsons, who was dropped in reaching eight before settling down to take the score to 48 when Sussex made the breakthrough 15 minutes before lunch. Ted Bowley "captured Parsons' wicket with a great puzzler". In other words, he was bowled.

His replacement Len Bates, who was born on the Edgbaston ground before eventually retiring to Sussex, was dropped on nought before lunch, by which time Cox was into his mammoth spell from the Town End. It didn't take him long into the afternoon when he returned to the attack at 2.45pm to start causing havoc.

With the total on 60, Wyatt was caught by a back-pedalling Jacko Watson running from mid-off, bringing Newhavenborn all-rounder Willie Quaife, a close friend of Cox's, to the wicket. Quaife and Bates began a partnership which was to take the score to 171, Bates collaring Cox for six to bring up Warwickshire's 150.

Cox broke the partnership when Bates played on for 77 after a stand lasting 75 minutes and by now "The Guv'nor" was well into his stride. He knocked back Norman Partridge's middle stump and with the score on 199 came the wicket that gave him most pleasure, perhaps, as Quaife's off peg was sent back.

"It beat me all the way and the ball went on with the arm," recalled Quaife. "But I would rather be bowled by my old pal George than anyone else." Quaife, at 54, was older than Cox and the pair had been opponents since the first match between the counties in 1905 when Cox dismissed Quaife for just one.

Now the fun started. As the wicket began to lose its moisture so the ball began to grip and turn sharply and Warwickshire's innings ground to a halt. Cox sent down ten maidens in 11 overs either side of tea and eventually the pressure told. Alf Croom was taken at slip, Norman Kilner and Jack Smart stumped as they came down the pitch and William Peare's middle stump was knocked back. Warwickshire were all out for 257, Cox having taken 8-56 in 38.4 overs, 19 of them maidens.

"The well-set out enclosure was packed, and at times there appeared to be insufficient seats," reported the *Sussex Daily News*. "Nothing could have suited the crowd so well as to see the local veteran George Cox take the honours with a brilliant feat of bowling. He was loudly cheered on conclusion of the Warwickshire innings."

Sussex lost Bowley in the hour's play before stumps and when the game resumed on Monday morning there was the highly unusual sight of Colonel Watson in the field for the opposition after Wyatt's return to the ground was delayed for an hour. He got a closer view than perhaps he would have liked of a Sussex batting collapse. There was still plenty in the wicket for the bowlers and Quaife's leg breaks brought him three wickets – including Cox for a duck – and at 148-8 Sussex looked certain to concede a hefty first-innings deficit.

They were rescued by a ninth-wicket stand between Harry Parks and Jack Holmes, the latter having come in when Sussex were 94-4 after two dismissals without addition to the score. Holmes began to accelerate and with his partner defending doggedly at the other end they took the score to 205 before Parks was dismissed.

But last man "Tich" Cornford, who had little pretensions as a batsman, proved just as obdurate as Parks and the pair took Sussex's total close to parity "before a single to Holmes made the scores a tie which was greeted by a round of cheers. A minute later, when Holmes drove Partridge to the boundary, there was a fine scene of enthusiasm." Holmes eventually fell for 87 but he had helped give his side a lead, albeit a slender one of just four runs.

Warwickshire went in again after tea and Wyatt and Parsons posted 50 in just 32 minutes as they looked to set up a last-day declaration. It wasn't long before Colonel Watson was calling Cox into the attack. "In this game George showed all his old wiles," recalled Watson. "His variation of pace and a fair amount of spin made him absolutely unplayable."

A stand of 72 in 72 minutes was ended by Cox when Wyatt edged to Cornford behind the stumps and before the close

Cox had taken 5-38 from 20 overs, seven of them maidens in an unbroken post-tea spell.

Parsons, shortly after reaching 50, was bowled "so curiously that for some time he did not realise what had happened". The pitch was now benign but Cox sensed nervousness and unease among the batsmen. Santall propped forward, overbalanced as the ball fizzed past the outside edge and Cornford did the rest.

At 121, Quaife was dismissed by his old pal for the second time in the match and before the close Kilner had lost his off stump without scoring. The crowd had been swelled after tea by hundreds of schoolboys, paying sixpence to see the final session, and once again Cox left the field to thunderous applause from the ring.

If the first two days had stretched credibility it was nothing compared to events on the third day as Cox completed what is still, 86 years later, the best match analysis in Sussex's history and the county secured a thrilling victory in the final over.

Rain was around again, but the threat of downpours seemed to help make the drama even more compelling. The home side, who had hoped to make further quick inroads into the Warwickshire batting, were kept off the field until 12.30pm by a heavy shower. When they resumed on 127-6 Croom and Bates added nine runs before Bates became Cox's sixth victim of the second innings, caught at mid-off, after making 30 in exactly 100 minutes.

Croom and Smart counter-attacked for a while and put on 39 in 36 minutes before Cox snared Smart shortly before lunch and then took his eighth wicket with the second ball after the resumption when Mayer lost his off stump. Peare did his best to hold things up "crouching cross-wise in front of the wicket, holding his bat in front of him as he strove his level best to withstand the veteran."

Cox eventually bowled him for a duck – the ninth time he had hit the stumps in the match. He took his sweater and walked off with match figures of 17-106 from 75.3 overs, 36 of which had been maidens. His second innings return of 9-50 has been bettered only seven times in the county's history. Bert Wensley had prevented The Guv'nor from taking all ten wickets.

Once again the crowd showed their appreciation for Old George. Nearly 31 years after his debut for the county he had produced one of the greatest bowling performances in Sussex's history. "The enthusiastic greeting the veteran had when the Sussex team left the field at the conclusion of the Warwickshire innings will not readily be forgotten," wrote Leather Hunter in the *Sussex Daily News*, adding a dash of colour to another lengthy and somewhat turgid account of the day's play.

It was often said by those who witnessed Cox's remarkable performance – and he never denied it himself – that his success came as a result of delivering the ball with a high arm action against a backdrop of dark trees at the Town End. As Quaife made his way back to the pavilion for the second time he smiled at his nemesis. "That one turned a bit quickly George. Must have pitched on a dandelion," was the equally dry response from his tormentor.

John Marshall, one of the many writers who chronicled the club's history, wrote of Cox's feats: "He had the batsmen shuffling from unease to helpfulness, getting an edge on it – or sometimes not even an edge at all – and leaving them baffled and bewildered. Varying his pace with his old skill – his faster one still had a bit of bite too – he imparted a disconcerting amount of spin."

Among the spectators was young George. The ball, which was presented to Cox later in the season during a presentation at the County Ground, became a treasured heirloom at the family home.

When the applause had died down and George was putting his feet up and his pipe on, Sussex set about scoring 174 for victory at 2.40pm. Only 21 runs had been made when rain drove the players off and it wasn't until 3.45pm that they could resume. Now time was of the essence.

Warwickshire's attack wasn't the strongest on the county circuit but in Wyatt they had a bowler capable of exploiting a drying pitch. With successive deliveries he dismissed Wensley and Ted Bowley after they had added 76 for the second wicket.

With 33 minutes remaining and 51 needed Harold Gilligan was joined by Tommy Cook. "Gilligan, blind to risk, straightaway went for the bowling and right heartily the ring applauded," wrote the *Sussex Daily News*. In ten minutes they added 19 and at one stage Cook loaned his partner his bat after his own split to save precious seconds waiting for a replacement to come down from the dressing room. "Jacko" Watson scored 19 in 13 balls and his replacement Holmes was waiting at the gate when Watson was dismissed with ten minutes remaining to get ten runs.

Together with Cook they scampered ones and twos before, off what was the first ball of the final over, Holmes late-cut Mayer to collect the winning runs. Perhaps it would have completed the tale had Cox been at the wicket when victory was secured but he remained in the dressing room with his pads on.

To bowl 75 overs was some effort for the 52-year-old, even for someone like Cox who was the fittest pro in the side after Tommy Cook, who played football for Brighton & Hove Albion, and certainly more battle-hardened than the Sussex amateurs. But he was back at Horsham the next day for the game against Gloucestershire and to the amazement of most, perhaps even himself, he took 6-45 in the first innings of a rain-affected match which ended in a draw.

Gilligan recalled "a game more reminiscent of country house than county cricket" and said: "George took six wickets in their first innings bringing up his aggregate for three innings to 23. The strain of so great a performance left its mark on him, and anno domini played its part afterwards," he said. To use George's own words 'If I had another pair of legs, some of them would have to answer for it.'"

Cox played in 19 more Championship games that year and by the end of it had sent down 877 overs, taking 82 wickets at 20.42. Only Tate, with 106 victims at 15.83, had a better summer for Sussex.

Two years later at the age of 54 Cox played in his 618th and final game for the county, fittingly on home turf at Horsham against Hampshire. He went wicket-less in both innings and scored four runs in his only visit to the crease batting at number eight. In 22 matches at Horsham he took 83 wickets at 16.50.

When he retired at the end of the season, ending a career which had spanned 34 summers, he had taken 1,810 wickets for Sussex at 22.83. Only Tate (2,211) has ever taken more and their place as the county's all-time top two is never likely to be bettered. In 1905 he took 164 wickets – a then county record – while his spectacular performance at Horsham in the twilight of his career was not the only occasion when he returned spectacular analyses. He had figures of 7-8 at Hove against Derbyshire in 1920 and a year later he took 5-0 in six overs against Somerset at Weston-super-Mare and bagged eight in an innings on six occasions. Once, playing for MCC Club and Ground, he took all ten wickets against the Royal Navy.

His batting was often overlooked but he was a more than capable lower-middle order hitter and was good enough to make an unbeaten 167 against Hampshire at Chichester in 1906, one of two hundreds for the county.

Old George had always been interested in coaching, not just teaching the game to his son in the fields near Warnham. He made four trips to South Africa and one to India during his playing career so it was no surprise when he became Sussex's coach. He died in 1949, ironically while visiting his sister in hospital in Dorking, aged 75.

There seems little doubt that his reputation as a hard-bitten professional, who doled out praise and platitudes sparingly, is not undeserved as his own son, who went on to serve Sussex magnificently in the 1940s and 1950s, would testify. He was a man of few words but his physical stature earned respect from both fellow pros and the jazz-hatters in the Sussex dressing room. He had high standards and demanded the same of his team-mates. When he turned to coaching, the young pros at Hove soon learned who was boss.

He was also a magnificent bowler who in his prime in the early years of the 20th century ought perhaps to have played for England. It was unfortunate that the peak of his career coincided with that of Kent's Colin Blythe and Wilfred Rhodes, of Yorkshire, a pair of gifted slow left-armers who would play 77 Tests between them.

George Cox had a fine, repeatable action and a deceptive change of pace. Arthur Gilligan, who was his captain for much of his career after the First World War, was unstinting in his praise when he asked to assess a player on whom he came to rely so much not just for his ability but his tactical nous and utter professionalism in every aspect of his game and the way he approached it.

"To George I owed a tremendous lot," said Gilligan. "He was one of the very best fighters I have ever known and I always gloried in having him on my side, especially when there was the possibility of a tight finish. His advice was always sound and he helped me more than I can adequately describe.

"Some of the side christened him 'the old warhorse' and for his years he was an absolute marvel. When we were having a good old leather hunt and our bowling had been knocked to every part of the field I used to look around in desperation to know whom to put on. Suddenly, I would catch George's eye and with that broad smile covering his sunny face he would come up to me and say 'what about me having another turn.' 'All right George, and God bless you' was my reply time and time again.

"As a senior professional he set very high standards to the others, instilling in them the best traditions of an English gentleman. George had a commanding personality and his influence on the team was a great one. I think he was one of the most loyal servants Sussex has ever had."

As epitaphs go, not bad. It might even have brought a gentle smile to the Guv'nor's lips.

MURRAY GOODWIN

2008: Good Man, Goodwin

NO ONE COULD dispute the importance of Mushtaq Ahmed to the most successful period in Sussex's history. Three Championships would have been impossible without the leg-spinner's consistent contributions but not far behind in terms of his enduring influence on Sussex's golden decade is Murray Goodwin.

Born in Zimbabwe but raised in Western Australia, Goodwin had already been at the club for two years when Mushtaq arrived in 2003 to propel them to greatness. And Goodwin's name is written in Sussex folklore forever, of course, because it was he who hit the winning runs when the Championship was secured for the first time in 2003 and Goodwin went on to make 335 not out, then the highest score in Sussex's first-class history.

It was a record he then broke in 2009 when, fuelled by Guinness and flu remedies, he scored 344 not out against Somerset and famously remarked afterwards that "staying out there seemed a good way of sweating out my cold". In 2012 Goodwin left the county after 13 seasons and more than 20,000 runs. During that period there have been fewer more consistent batsmen throughout the county game, home-grown, overseas or Kolpak, as Goodwin has been classified for the last eight years.

His is a phenomenal record. At the start of 2012 he had scored over 22,000 runs for Sussex in all formats including 48 Championship hundreds placing him sixth on the all-time list. Only Chris Adams (11) has made more List A centuries than his ten in an aggregate of 6,312 runs in 50-over and 40-over cricket while he is the only Sussex player to score two centuries in Twenty20 matches, the most recent in 2011 coming at the age of 38 when most batsmen of his age have long since given up the shortest format of the game.

But when the cognoscenti in the deckchairs at Hove start their rheumy-eyed reminiscences about what was Goodwin's best ever knock that record-breaker on a shirt-front at Taunton rarely gets a mention. Instead, after remembering the pull-shot off Phil DeFreitas which won the Championship for the first time, the debate invariably turns to an unbeaten 87 against Nottinghamshire in 2008 which almost single-handedly ensured that Chris Adams' reign as the most successful captain in Sussex's history ended with yet another trophy, the Pro40 title which Goodwin sealed with a six off the last ball at Trent Bridge, his favourite English venue away from Hove. "In the circumstances, I don't think I have ever played a better innings for Sussex," he believes.

Back in 2008 English cricket was undergoing another period of painful introspection over the make-up of the domestic fixture-list. The counties had voted to bring in a second Twenty20 competition so something had to give in a congested calendar and the Pro40, which had been played under the auspices of various sponsors since the John Player County League started in 1969, was ripe for the chop even though counties had reported increased attendances for 40-over fixtures, mainly from Twenty20 audiences exploring a slightly longer version of the game.

At the start of the 2008 season the ECB outlined the conclusions of the Schofield Report – the latest think-tank led by Ken Schofield, the head honcho of the European Golf Tour, and commissioned to look into the fixture list. Its recommendations were batted back and forth between Lord's and the shires before being quietly shelved but not after they announced that the Pro40 would be culled after 2009 in favour of a second Twenty20 competition.

The governing body's research (mostly carried out at Twenty20 games) revealed an appetite from the public for more of the same. But a year later there was no second Twenty20 and it was 50-over cricket rather than 40-over matches which bit the dust, even though 50 was the duration of limited-overs encounters played at international level.

Goodwin says he and the rest of his team-mates were fairly diffident about the one-day format. "We all thought and still do that there is too much cricket played but most of us didn't prefer 50 or 40 overs. I liked it because it's less fielding time but ten overs to be honest didn't make a huge difference and being good over 50 overs didn't always mean you'd be competitive over 40."

To prove his point, Sussex had finished bottom of their group in the Friends Provident Trophy in 2008, with just one win in eight games two years after essentially the same group of players had won the final at Lord's. Their performances in the Twenty20 Cup were not much better either with eight defeats from ten games in 2008 coming a year after they had lost their semi-final to Kent.

In 2007 Adams led Sussex to their third Championship in five years but there was a sense the following season that their golden era was quietly coming to an end. After hobbling through 33 overs against Lancashire in a Championship game at Hove at the beginning of July, Mushtaq Ahmed underwent knee surgery for the second time in two months and after making one more appearance, against the same county at Old Trafford, in early August he called it a day.

Adams probably would have stepped down as captain had Lancashire rather than his side won the Championship on that dramatic final day in 2007. Instead he stayed on and was able to step down on his terms and with another trophy in his hands. But he had made up his mind to give up the captaincy in June in favour of Mike Yardy and finally made the announcement a few minutes after Goodwin's stupendous innings at Trent Bridge. "To be honest what happened after that day is a bit of a blur," said Goodwin. "If Grizz announced his retirement I don't remember it – I probably wasn't listening anyway!"

In the Championship, Sussex won just two four-day games and only stayed up by five points. Only one batsman passed 1,000 runs – the ever-reliable Goodwin who, at 35, still felt at the peak of his powers. He finished the four-day season with 1,343 runs at 58.39 including six hundreds – the same number as the rest of the 19 players put together.

"I think it helped that until 2007 I played competitively in Australia as well during the winter before coming to Sussex," said Goodwin. "It made sure the competitive edge was still there when I came over to England and 2007 was my last year playing in Australia at State level.

"Those years from 2003 to 2008 were probably my peak years for Sussex. After that I had to become even more self-motivated which has been hard work, but I have always loved being among the guys and trying to do well for them and for myself."

When Sussex started their Pro40 campaign at Arundel against Somerset on 20th July it wasn't without any great expectations of challenging for the title. Their perilous position in the Championship was the priority but on a blissfully sunny Sunday afternoon a crowd of 5,000 witnessed what would have been, in any other year, the best one-day innings of the season as Matt Prior scored 137 off 123 balls to lead Sussex to their target of 243 with two balls to spare.

With only eight games in the competition there was little room for error but a fortnight later Sussex got a fortunate break when the umpires abandoned the game at Horsham against Worcestershire because of rain. Three more balls would have brought a result: a Worcestershire victory unless Sussex had scored 11 runs. Only Luke Wright, whose 4-56 were his best figures in the competition for four years, could consider it a good day.

Two days later the game against Gloucestershire at Cheltenham was abandoned without a ball bowled. Played three, won one. There was even less margin for error now.

Sussex headed straight to Old Trafford to start Mushtaq's last Championship game the following day. Fortunately, a final-day washout meant their onward journey to Durham for the next Pro40 game the following day was conducted at a more leisurely pace. Their pursuit of a revised target of 224 from 38 overs was supervised by Prior who made 79 from 83 balls. Even then, with one run needed off three balls, Sussex only got home with a scrambled single off the final delivery.

Halfway through the group stage, Goodwin had only contributed 30 runs and his form did not improve in Sussex's next game where he made three as Sussex were hammered by Hampshire by 66 runs. Fortunately, none of the other eight counties were taking a stranglehold on the division but the points gained from those two no-results effectively meant another win. Victories in their next two matches, both at Hove, would keep them in the hunt for honours.

Goodwin made his fourth half-century of the season in limited overs cricket against Lancashire under the Hove lights when his unbeaten 58 on a turgidly slow surface guided Sussex to a four-wicket win. Later that week he scored an unbeaten hundred against Nottinghamshire in the Championship. "I have tended to finish the season strongly and that was one of those years. Things started to go quite well," he said.

Four counties had realistic ambitions of winning the Pro40 as the penultimate round of fixtures began. On 10th September Nottinghamshire blew the chance to go clear at the top when they lost by one run at Trent Bridge to already-relegated Lancashire. The following evening Sussex knew that victory over Middlesex would set up a last-day title decider against the Outlaws.

By now the Sussex bowlers knew how to bowl on the slow pitches predominant at Hove. They dismissed Middlesex for 165 and Goodwin then produced another gem of an innings – 54 not out from 72 balls – to ease them to a five-wicket win with 22 balls to spare.

The First Division table was so tight that Durham began their final game in danger of finishing third from bottom and facing a play-off. Instead they beat Gloucestershire and ended up third. But the game at Trent Bridge was effectively a final in itself – winner takes all.

The omens were mixed. Two years earlier Sussex had gone to Nottingham knowing a win would secure the 40-over title and lost. At least they won the Championship game a few days later and with it their second title. But if there was any pre-match nerves among Adams' men they certainly didn't affect Goodwin. Trent Bridge? Nottingham? He couldn't get enough of the place.

On his first visit there in 2000, in what turned out to be his 19th and last Test appearance, Goodwin had made a chanceless 148 not out and his third Test hundred for Zimbabwe against an England attack comprising Andy Caddick, Darren Gough, ex-Sussex seamer Ed Giddins, Chris Schofield (no relation to Ken) and Andrew Flintoff. Raised on the bouncy pitches of Perth, Goodwin cut and pulled with impunity but rain robbed Zimbabwe of what would have been a famous victory.

"We were in the driving seat and I made some runs," remembers Goodwin with typical modesty. "But there were a lot of issues at the time in Zimbabwean cricket although I didn't think at the time it would be my last Test. I got my name on the honours board in the pavilion at Trent Bridge alongside some great players. Whenever I went back I always checked it was still there and who the most recent additions to the board were."

Nottingham, with its big student population, is always a popular place with visiting teams. "It's a place that has always had a good feel to it for me. Most of the Notts lads were quite sociable down the years and I loved going out there for a few beers," says Goodwin.

Trent Bridge itself soon grew in appeal. In 2001 – his first season for Sussex – Goodwin made 115 in the first innings and then a maiden double-hundred in the second as he and Richard Montgomerie put on 372 for the first wicket, the fourth-highest partnership in the county's history. Between 2001 and 2011 Goodwin has scored 1,025 runs in all competitions at Trent Bridge at an average of 73.21, including five hundreds.

Goodwin was also a batsman who tended to get better as the season unfolded. Arriving in England's spring chill from the warmth of Perth was something he never really got used to during his long career with Sussex. "I have always needed a few innings to get going, to get accustomed to the light as much as anything else," he admits. Goodwin has scored 22 of his hundreds in all formats for Sussex in August and September.

He arrived at Trent Bridge that bright Sunday morning of 14th September in good form. As well as those two half-centuries which had revived his side's Pro40 hopes he had scored Championship hundreds in two of his previous four games.

What he, Adams and the rest of the Sussex team discovered when they checked the wicket on their way to practice was not a surprise. He says: "It was a used pitch, which in itself was not unusual at that time of the year, but it was very dry. We knew it would turn and we felt a score of around 240 would be competitive."

A warm day had persuaded around 200 Sussex supporters to make the trip to Nottingham in a crowd of around 6,000. Most, of course, were there to see their side try and win their first one-day league title for 19 years and when it was announced that Chris Read had won the toss and decided to bat there was even a ripple of applause from the members' area. "It wasn't going to decide the game, but it was definitely a good toss to win," remembered Goodwin.

With Mushtaq hobbling off into retirement Sussex recruited another Pakistani for the final few weeks of the season. Mohammad Sami was not a leg-spinner. Instead he bowled quickly and could swing the ball both ways. "He gave the attack some bite," said Goodwin.

Sami shared the new ball with James Kirtley and soon made a breakthrough when he bowled Graeme Swann, who was Nottinghamshire's pinch-hitter, for a duck. Kirtley had Mark Wagh caught in the covers with the score on 19 but Will Jefferson rebuilt the innings with Samit Patel in a stand of 46 for the third wicket. Patel, though, had a let-off on eight when he top-edged a pull off Kirtley towards Sami at long leg. The fielder seemed to lose the flight of the ball in the sun and it dropped a yard short of him. "It wasn't an easy chance by any means but he didn't seem to pick it up at all," said Goodwin.

It was to prove a costly miss. Patel, also reprieved on 59 when Mike Yardy shelled a sharp return catch, went on to make 78 from 82 balls and added 82 in 16 overs with the South African import Ashwell Prince for the fourth wicket before Rory Hamilton-Brown, who was getting some sharp turn with his off-breaks, stalled the momentum by dismissing both batsmen in successive overs.

Nottinghamshire regrouped and scored 46 runs in the last five overs, Andre Adams swatting the last ball of the innings off Kirtley into the pavilion for six. Sussex would need to score 227, which was gettable but not easy given that Swann and Patel offered a greater threat on a turning pitch than the Sussex spinners.

The reply didn't start well. Sussex would have wanted Matt Prior, opening with Yardy, and number three Luke Wright to take advantage of a hard ball and the fielding restrictions but both were back in the dressing room with 32 runs on the board as Darren Pattinson struck twice.

Rebuilding was required so Yardy – who had made his England ODI debut on the same ground two years earlier – and Adams took the score to 87 in the space of ten overs before Patel bowled Yardy for 53. By now Swann and Patel were bowling in tandem – off-breaks and slow left-arm – and as the pressure to maintain a scoring rate of 5.57 per over mounted Goodwin walked out to join his captain.

"It wasn't looking good. We were behind the rate and the ball was turning for Swann and Patel a lot," said Goodwin. "I remember saying to Chris Read that whatever happens we'll still have a good time tonight, we will still have a beer. He replied that we would do well to win it from the position we were in at that stage which was quite a confident thing to say because we were only three wickets down."

Soon, though, Sussex were eight wickets down. Adams, trying to force off the back foot, was bowled by Swann, Dwayne Smith was bowled through the gate, head in the air, by Swann while both Carl Hopkinson and Hamilton-Brown were beaten in the flight and stumped by at least a yard. When Robin Martin-Jenkins mis-timed a pull and was caught at mid-on Sussex had gone from 105-3 to 130-8 and Swann and Patel had helped themselves to a share of six wickets.

"What was poor that day was how we batted against the turning ball," remembers Goodwin. "The annoying thing was that we had some good players of spin in that side but it is amazing what pressure does. We just didn't pick the right balls to attack.

"I was quite relaxed, though, for some reason. There was no pressure really when we were eight down. We were losing wickets but I always felt that someone would stay with me to form a partnership that might get us going again.

"But you do need luck as well and I think I had some that day. I played a couple of sweeps that got top-edges which fell short of fielders but I was just trying to be really selective, especially against Swann and Patel. I had to take on the responsibility and make sure I didn't lose my wicket and hopefully build a partnership with someone.

"I was just hoping the spinners would bowl out before we'd lost to be honest because I felt more confident that our tail-end guys would do better facing the seamers. Mark Ealham came back on and we got into him a bit and although Pattinson and Shreck were good bowlers they weren't going to get you out through sheer speed."

Number ten Sami walked out with exactly ten overs to go and 97 runs needed. Sami was not the worst number ten in the world. In 121 international appearances for Pakistan he had made 49 in a Test and 46 in an ODI so he had ability. The problem Goodwin faced was simply one of communication.

He said: "Sami's English wasn't the best. He understood basic stuff and I imagine Mushy probably taught him a few phrases but it wasn't easy. When he came in all I kept telling him was to hit straight. I just told him that if the ball was there to hit you hit it – he was quite a strong guy and he had a good eye. But I said if it's straight you make sure you don't go across the line and risk being an lbw candidate. Did he understand? I don't think so but he kept nodding so maybe he did."

Sussex's cause, of course, must have appeared utterly hopeless to the supporters in the ground and those watching live on TV at home but while Goodwin, a rescuer of so many seemingly lost causes over the years, was there hope sprung eternal. In New York City, two Sussex supporters, Paul Moran and Jon Filby, were following the game on BBC Radio Nottingham's internet coverage.

Jon was receiving texts from his brother Bill in the ground. "It didn't look good and when the eighth wicket went down Jon said 'that's it, finished. Let's go'," Paul said. Central Park and a Talking Heads concert in the New York sunshine beckoned. "Then we thought 'Oh well it's Muzza. Let's just listen to one more over, see what happens and then we will leave anyway'."

Sami hit a six off Swann and with Goodwin starting to warm to his task slowly but surely the partnership built. "At eight wickets down I got the sense they had taken their foot off the gas," remembered Goodwin. "For five or six overs they relaxed and we saw off Patel and Swann and the seamers came back on. I hit Ealham and Pattinson for six and suddenly we had got down to the last four overs needing 41 runs to win and that was probably the first point at which I thought we might have a chance.

"It's happened to me so many times in my career. Once you lose that intensity as a fielding side when you think a match is done and dusted it can be very hard to pick it back up again.

"Once Sami settled in he looked OK. He had a bit of luck too. He could have chopped on a couple of times against

Swann and he edged it over the inner field a couple of times. I just kept walking down the pitch telling him to hit straight and I think the message had started to get through. By then when I asked him where he was going to hit the ball he just kept saying 'straight, straight.' It was the answer I was hoping for."

Sussex needed 26 when the penultimate over began and got ten of them off Ealham. They needed 16 off the final over, which was entrusted to the tall Cornishman Shreck from the Radcliffe Road End for the first time in the competition that season. Nottinghamshire were still favourites but the batsmen had the short leg-side boundary on the Fox Road side of Trent Bridge to attack.

Across the Atlantic they were feeling the tension too. "Sixteen runs from six balls to be delivered by the up until now parsimonious Shreck was still a big ask," remembered Paul Moran. "Jon was more anxious than a vasectomy patient who'd just noticed the surgeon was cross-eyed. The internet was costing us an outrageous $12.95 an hour but Jon's infectious enthusiasm had transformed me into a big Sussex fan for the day."

For the Sussex players gathered on the dressing-room balcony it was hard to know whether to believe or accept that a brave effort was probably going to fall short. "I'd written my 'well done Nottinghamshire' speech in my head," admitted Adams.

Goodwin, though, seemed to be relishing the situation. "There was a short boundary on one side and that was massively in their mind and I was happy that Shreck was bowling too because Pattinson still had an over left and I thought he would have been a better bet. But Shreck had done that job all season for them in one-day cricket so it was horses for courses I suppose. Look, 16 runs was still a lot to get but I just had a feeling that we were on a roll, that momentum was with us and if the luck held we might just pull it off."

Goodwin, on strike, clipped the first ball backward of square for four but could only take a single to backward square-leg off the second. "I hit that one straight out of the guts but it went straight to the fielder on the boundary."

Sami was now on strike. "Play straight" urged his partner in another brief mid-pitch pow-wow but the force was clearly with Sami. He went for broke and a big outside edge flew past the diving Read and down to the third-man boundary. Nine off three balls scored, seven to win. A single off the fourth delivery got the equation down to six from two but Goodwin knew that if the scores were tied and Sussex were level on points at the top they would take the title by dint of having won more games.

Goodwin hit the fifth ball to the deep cover boundary. "Ashwell Prince was fielding and Sami should have been run out going for the second run but Prince was right on the rope instead of being ten yards in to stop twos, especially with me on strike, and he threw it to my end," he said. "If he'd aimed it at the non-striker's end Sami would have been a gonner."

Three to win, although the denouement was still a few moments away as Read and Shreck gathered in mid-pitch to discuss their options. Goodwin said: "I was trying to hear what they were saying but Sami was well pumped up by now and kept talking to me so I told him to shut up so I could try and pick up what they were discussing. I remember Shreck saying 'what if he laps me?' Fine leg was up and it was a short boundary so he was worried I might go across my stumps and try to clip him fine.

"So I guessed he would go offside because he was concerned about being lapped. I just wanted to hit it straight which was my strength. When he ran in I went deep into my crease towards off stump because I felt if he missed his yorker I could squeeze it past point for four or hit it back past him.

"I swung but I didn't quite get it in the screws. I hit it OK but it wasn't one where I knew as soon as I'd hit it that it would go for six. I looked over towards the long-on boundary and saw Andre Adams put his hands up to catch it and then just as quickly he put them down again as if to say 'that's gone' and it ended up about ten yards over the rope. For a second I thought I'd hit it down his throat and then in the next second it was 'no, it's gone!' I couldn't believe how far I had hit it to be honest."

Neither could anyone else. With the ball in the air and seemingly heading straight to Adams the Nottinghamshire fans were on their feet. Seconds later Goodwin was being lifted off his feet by Sami, whose 32 not out off 30 balls had helped make the seemingly impossible possible. A six off the last ball had won the game and Sussex were champions in the most dramatic way possible.

Goodwin raised his hands, bat in one hand, helmet in the other and briefly took it all in having scored 87 runs in 64 balls with three sixes and six fours. He said: "I turned around and our dressing room was going absolutely wild and the next thing I knew our Academy Director Keith Greenfield, who had come up to watch, was running onto the pitch and giving me a big hug and kiss. Sami just kept saying 'unbelievable,

unbelievable, unbelievable'." For a man of few words, he had summed up a remarkable day pretty well.

Over in New York the BBC Radio Nottingham commentators were describing Shreck's run-up to the crease to deliver the final ball. Then silence. In the building excitement, Messrs Moran and Filby had failed to notice that their hour of internet connection was running out. The line went dead just as Shreck was leaping into his delivery stride.

"Noooooooooooooooooooooo!" said Paul. "Quick Jon, where's your phone? He didn't need to search for it...it was ringing. Jon switched on the speakerphone, it was his brother Bill. There was cheering coming down the line. Muzza had done it with a six smashed over long on. Storybook stuff."

The trophy presented and champagne sprayed the Sussex players returned to their dressing room to continue the celebrations and absorb the news that Adams was stepping down as captain. But the combination of what he had achieved and where he had achieved it meant Goodwin was soon partying the night away in Nottingham.

He said: "We were staying over because we were travelling onto a Championship game up at Durham. All I had eaten that day was breakfast and a piece of fruit after the warm-ups which was not normal for me, although I don't like playing with a full stomach.

"I had a big night but I paid for it. The aftermath came a few days later when I got sick and had to miss a day of the Durham game recovering in bed."

A year later Sussex retained their crown and once again the drama unfolded on the final day. Victory at Worcester would have given them the title without having to rely on other results but Sussex rarely do straightforward, as their supporters will attest.

Sure enough Sussex, with only six survivors from Trent Bridge, made a mess of a relatively straightforward target of 215 and were bowled out for 165. The game over, the big screen at New Road began transmitting live pictures of Durham's pursuit of 243 to beat Somerset and keep the title at Hove.

Goodwin said: "We had packed up and were getting ready to leave when someone said that Durham still had a chance. It was a bit surreal, standing on the balcony there and watching it with all our supporters. We were lucky. We didn't play smart cricket, underestimated Worcestershire and played some silly shots. But Durham had an unbelievable win against Somerset."

Back-to-back champions but nothing will ever beat the drama of 2008. Goodwin said: "I have been fortunate to play some good one-day innings in my career and not just for Sussex, but that was one of the best. Of course I didn't think we could win it from the position we were in and if I'm honest I under-estimated Sami's capabilities as a batsman. He did a wonderful job.

"People still come up to me now, four years later, and talk about that day. I will never forget it and I hope Sami won't either. He was gone again a few weeks after that game but I hope he still remembers it like I do."

IAN GOULD

1986: Tearing Up The Script

IAN GOULD MADE 18 limited-overs appearances for England in the first half of 1983 and played in the World Cup. Far greater recognition on the international stage followed more than 20 years later when, four years after he joined the first-class umpires list, Gould officiated in an ODI at the Oval between England and Sri Lanka.

Since then his umpiring career has taken him all over the world. As an English umpire he gets very few opportunities to stand on home soil and only once has he officiated at his favourite ground, Lord's. It is a good job, then, that Gould, or "Gunner" as he is known to everyone in the game, has some fond memories of headquarters from his playing days.

Taken on to the Middlesex staff in 1975, he had six seasons with the county but left in 1981 to join Sussex because of a lack of opportunity at Lord's. Within five years he was captaining what was regarded as a disparate group of world-class cricketers, emerging players and Sussex-raised youngsters to victory against the odds in the 1986 NatWest final, only the second trophy the county won during a decade when a talented squad failed to fulfill what was expected of them, not least by themselves.

The run to the final against Lancashire featured some of the most eventful matches in Sussex history. And it all started when Gould walked out for the toss before the first-round game against Suffolk and discovered he did not have a coin. Gould remembers what happened as if it was yesterday: "I turned round to Peter Eaton, the groundsman, and asked him for a coin. Peter was a lovely man but you didn't see him with money too often and when he dug into his pockets all he had was a two-pence piece. Anyway, we needed to win the toss because it wasn't one of his best wickets and we did. And from then on I kept the 2p with me and it turned out to be our lucky charm."

Of course Sussex's run to the final wasn't all down to Gould calling correctly before each of their four games they played to get to Lord's. They played some fine cricket too as the season began to gather momentum after an uncertain first couple of months. On a horrible Headingley pitch they overcame a strong Yorkshire side thanks to a brilliant counter-attacking innings by their captain before overcoming all manner of distractions, mostly weather-related, in the semi-final at New Road against Worcestershire. Then in the final they tore up the script on what was Clive Lloyd's last big game.

Even more remarkably, they did so without the services of a recognised slow bowler. These days it would be unthinkable for a side to play in any of the one-day formats – 20, 40 or 50 overs – without a spinner. Most play two or sometimes three, even in Twenty20.

Back in 1986 David Standing bowled 12 overs of his part-time off breaks in the first-round win and five overs in the subsequent victory over Glamorgan, but apart from that Gould was only able to use his seam attack, albeit a very handy one headed by the leonine Imran Khan, who was acknowledged as one of the best all-rounders in the world, and the powerful South African Garth le Roux.

Although Gould was an established member of the side when the 1986 season started he was not exactly obvious captaincy material. Old Etonian John Barclay had led the county since 1981 and almost took Sussex to their first Championship that year. But by 1986 he was struggling with a finger injury, caused not from bowling but from years of trying to fend off the new ball in his role as opening batsman in the Championship side.

Slow left-armer Chris Waller had left the club at the end of 1985 to take up a coaching appointment at Surrey and although Barclay was fit enough to lead the team at the start of the new season the injury became too troublesome and after a John Player League game against Somerset on 1st June he stepped down. Gould had already led the side in the John Player League a couple of times that year and although he complemented the more cerebral Barclay well in his role as vice-captain leading the side was another matter altogether, although Barclay had no doubts he was up to the task.

"Ian did a wonderful job when he suddenly found himself holding the reigns," Barclay said. "He combined a deep knowledge of the game from behind the stumps with a natural, punchy panache to drive everyone on. He was possibly the most naturally gifted individual in the side and when he allowed himself total freedom he could turn the course of a match on his own which he did in the quarter-final at Headingley, a match I will never forget."

Gould's appointment was made official early in June but he hardly inherited a settled squad. Both le Roux and the emerging young opening batsman Neil Lenham broke fingers within a week of each other (not for the last time in Lenham's case) while Adrian Jones, the fastest bowler on the staff after the two overseas players, was plagued by a knee problem and then sore toes caused, it turned out, by ill-fitting bowling boots.

Sussex had hinted at what they could be capable of in one-day cricket by emerging from a strong group to reach the quarter-finals of the Benson & Hedges Cup but they were well beaten by Middlesex by 84 runs with Gould bagging a duck.

In the John Player League Sussex had won three and lost three of their first six while the first seven Championship games had yielded just a solitary victory.

For the more genteel at Hove, whether sitting in the deckchairs or the committee room, the appointment of Gould as Barclay's successor was certainly a culture shock. With three initials and schooled at Eton, Barclay certainly fitted the bill as captain of the oldest first-class county. Slough-born Gould, who spoke with a Cockney accent and swore like a trooper, did not. He liked a pint or two and chain-smoked when he wasn't on the field and would often get through 30 cigarettes a day. But neither concerned themselves with snobbish trivialities and Gould was very much his own man.

"We had a very individualistic side," he says. "It was pretty simple really. I let the boys do their own thing and I respected their wisdom, certainly those guys who had played a bit. Imran and Garth were fantastic bowlers who knew what they wanted and I encouraged our batsmen to play their own way.

They were all pretty good, they knew their games. In one-day cricket I really enjoyed the cut and thrust of captaincy. Where I found it more difficult was in Championship matches. Those could be long days sometimes."

Gould's first Championship game after his appointment was confirmed could hardly have gone any worse. There was no Jones, le Roux or Lenham because of injury when Sussex faced a strong Essex side that went on to win the Championship that year at Valentines Park in Ilford. Ray Alikhan, who was to become one of the unlikely heroes of the NatWest triumph, made his debut batting at number eight while slow left-armer Andrew Bredin batted at 11 yet only bowled four overs in the first innings. Replying to Essex's 242, Sussex were 15-6 in their reply and although they recovered to make 112 they still lost by 69 runs. Jones returned for the next game against Worcestershire, which finished in a draw, but Sussex lost the John Player League match played on the Sunday.

When the NatWest Trophy campaign began at Hove on 25th June both Le Roux and Lenham were still missing. Having called correctly with Peter Eaton's 2p coin, Gould put Suffolk in. A seven-wicket win, after they had dismissed Suffolk cheaply, suggests it was an easy day for Sussex. Gould insists it was anything but.

"We could easily have lost that game. It was a used pitch which spun a lot," he said. "Trout (Barclay) wasn't fit of course so we had to play David Standing and he got us out of a hole with his offies. They lost an early wicket but they had a decent opener called Mike McEvoy who had played for Worcestershire and Essex and a good skipper, Simon Clements, and together they put on a few runs. Anyway, David came on and knocked McEvoy's off stump over and then he had Clements caught in the deep. After that we were always in control in the field."

When Sussex began their chase to score 109 Gould made the first of his major tactical change since becoming captain, sending out Rehan Alikhan to open the batting with Allan Green. It turned out to be a master-stroke on Gould's part.

He said: "Ray was one of the nicest men I've ever met in my life but he was also the bravest or stupidest I've ever come across in cricket. He could play the game but what I liked about him was that he was very brave and didn't mind getting hit. You have to remember in those days most counties had one or two very fine opening bowlers.

"Imran and Garth were sharp as we know but guys like Courtney Walsh were coming through and there were English bowlers who could go through the gears like Norman Cowans and Syd Lawrence.

"Ray didn't mind getting hit and he had the ideal temperament to open because even in one-day cricket his job would be to blunt the opposition's new-ball bowlers. The NatWest was 60 overs in those days so you could afford to build an innings, you didn't have to go out looking to blast it from ball one.

"I remember one game here against Gloucestershire in the Championship and Syd Lawrence was bowling like the clappers and screaming at Ray because he kept playing and missing. Syd was basically too good for him. He gave him a couple of bouncers so Ray just smiled, took his helmet off and put a white sunhat on instead!

"Opposition bowlers took him for a bit of a fool but the guys loved him. He would get hit everywhere but he is a bloke I would want in my team every day of the week. In the semi-final against Worcestershire he virtually saw off Neal Radford with the new ball single-handedly.

"If Radford bowled 72 balls at Ray I doubt if he hit ten of them. In those conditions Radford ought to have got seven wickets and if Ray had nicked one early on we'd have been gone – all over, beaten in the semi-finals."

The experiment was hardly a roaring success. Alikhan made a duck against a modest Suffolk attack but Sussex eased to victory by seven wickets thanks to an unbeaten 40 from Paul Parker.

By the time Sussex took on Glamorgan at Hove in the second round a fortnight later Lenham had recovered from injury and Alikhan found himself batting with the tail at number eight.

In that game Green scored the only hundred of the NatWest campaign as Sussex won by 29 runs. Green, born in Pulborough but educated at Brighton College, was arguably the most naturally gifted batsman in the side but by 1986 he was beginning to fall out of love with the game and in 1989 he had retired at the age of 29 after scoring more than 7,000 runs for Sussex during the decade.

"One of my biggest regrets as captain was not doing enough to help Allan," says Gould. "I regard him as one of the greatest players to play for Sussex. He batted so beautifully, he made it look so easy. I still see him now and ask him what went wrong and he doesn't know, it was just one of those things. If we'd had sports scientists in those days they would have been able to get their head round it and help Allan but he simply fell out of love with the game. He was a very fine player though and on the way to Lord's he played some wonderful innings for us."

Green scored 102 and Imran 54 and when Sussex defended a total of 269 their seamers did an outstanding job. Glamorgan's reply was going well at 107-1 but Colin Wells, on as first change, picked up John Hopkins and Hugh Morris while Andy Babington, in his second and final appearance in the competition that year, collected two wickets including a young Matt Maynard. Standing and Lenham did a solid job in the fill-in overs before Gold Award winner Imran returned to mop up the tail as Glamorgan were bowled out for 240 off the second ball of the final over.

Sussex's luck with home draws didn't hold. The quarter-final would be at Headingley at the end of July against Yorkshire and in the intervening three weeks Gould began to galvanise his side. They won three successive JPL games and then beat Worcestershire at Hove before losing to Surrey at Guildford in the County Championship. Le Roux returned after injury and picked up seven wickets in the two matches while Gould's persistence with Alikhan at the top of the order appeared to be paying off when he scored half-centuries in both innings against Worcestershire.

The side which played Yorkshire would remain unchanged all the way to Lord's: Alikhan, Green, Parker, Imran Khan, Alan Wells, Colin Wells, Gould, le Roux, Dermot Reeve, Tony Pigott and Jones. There was still no spinner of course, but a formidable seam attack and with le Roux back in the mix a strong lower middle-order.

When Gould arrived at Headingley on the morning of 30th July, having driven up when the Championship game at Guildford concluded the previous evening, he could not believe what he saw. "It was a shocking wicket," he recalls. The pitch had been used for the second Test against India six weeks earlier which the tourists won in just over three days. "Hammonds Sauce Works Band, playing in front of the Football Stand, was the indisputable success for England in the match," *Wisden* had reported.

"It was horribly uneven and to make it worse it was very overcast. At Headingley some days the clouds would just hover just above the ground and this was one of those days. On the first day we only played a bit because of rain," said Gould.

Barclay had travelled up with the squad and although he had no chance of playing he made a crucial intervention just before Gould went out for the toss.

He said: "I was hell-bent on fielding first and John, in that lovely way of his, said he didn't think I should be doing that because we need runs on the board. We thought anything around 180 would be a decent total so we batted but they clearly backed their seam attack, which was decent, to out-bowl ours which I often thought opposition sides underrated."

It was now that Gould played what he regards as his best innings for Sussex. Sussex were 86-6 when le Roux walked out to join his captain on the second day after much of the first had been lost to drizzle and bad light.

Gould recalls: "I had a lot of luck early on and then their captain David Bairstow had an absolute shocker and took the seamers off when they were all over us. Phil Carrick came on to bowl his left-arm spin and that took the pressure off us a bit. He only went for two runs an over but when they had us six down I think they thought they'd done the hard bit and they let us get away with it."

Riding their luck, Gould and le Roux added 115 for the seventh wicket before Gould fell for 88 from 80 balls, at the time his highest score in one-day cricket. "It was that sort of wicket where 88 felt like 140," he said.

Yorkshire's target was 214 but they never got close. "That was as well as I saw Sussex bowl in a one-day game during that era," says their captain. "We knocked them over for fun, absolute fun." At one stage Yorkshire had lost four wickets for one run. "Fergie (Carrick) got 54 but they were 96-7 by then and it was all over," he added.

Le Roux and Jones, bowling with sustained hostility, shared eight wickets as Yorkshire were bowled out for 125 in 38.3 overs. To add to their disappointment, the pitch was reported to Lord's as unfit by umpires Jack Birkenshaw and John Holder.

If the quarter-final had been plagued by bad weather it was nothing compared to the sight which greeted Gould and his players on the morning of Wednesday 13th August after they had made another cross-country dash, this time from Southampton, on the eve of the game for the semi-final.

The ground had been under water for much of the week and although a wan sun was now peering through the clouds Gould and his team knew they would be in for a long wait, even though the gates had opened and the ground was beginning to fill up with patient and good-natured spectators, several hundred of them from Sussex.

"Blimey – Worcester," he says. "We turned up and it looked like God's nightmare had arrived. The ground had been flooded and the pitch was wet. We were very lucky because Roy Palmer and Don Oslear were the umpires and they were sticklers for that sort of thing. In those days some umpires wouldn't worry too much if water had got under the covers and the run-ups were a bit damp. These days they'd never get away with it of course.

"They had three spinners in their side and we didn't have one so I was forever in their ear-holes about the conditions and, to their credit, they made sure it was fit before we eventually started."

The Worcestershire side included a young Graeme Hick. Bowled by Imran for one he did not exert much influence on proceedings but his father John certainly did. In an effort to help dry out the run-ups Hick senior suggested the ground-staff employ the same techniques he would use to dry out tobacco on his farm in Zimbabwe and soon parts of the square were covered by canopies with space heaters blasting out hot air underneath.

In an even more ingenious attempt to dry out the ground, Worcestershire summoned a local garage owner to hover over the outfield with his helicopter two or three feet above the grass while the downdraught from its rotor-blades sucked up the moisture.

"That was a complete waste of fuel," laughs Gould. "I don't think it made any difference but the heaters certainly did. I won the toss again and we naturally put them in but we didn't make a great start to be honest."

Both captains felt 150 would be a competitive total and when the game resumed the following day Worcestershire openers Tim Curtis and Damian D'Oliveira found the pace of Imran and le Roux coming nicely onto the bat. Worcestershire were 66-1 when Gould brought on Colin Wells and Dermot Reeve with immediate results. "They were unplayable," says Gould. "They took the pace off the ball, bowled cutters and got it to swing a little bit and suddenly the runs dried up."

Bowling a combined total of 17 overs for just 31 runs Worcestershire lost momentum and when Gould summoned Imran for another burst midway through the innings he quickly removed Hick, Phil Neale and Dipak Patel. Worcestershire slumped to 99-8 before making a partial recovery to 125 although there were still nine overs of their innings remaining when the last wicket fell.

Sussex were soon 31-3 in their reply but Alikhan blunted their seam attack and when he was fourth out on the Friday morning – the game having gone into a third day – he had made 41 and Sussex only needed another 23 runs. A five-wicket victory was achieved in the 49th over and Sussex were heading back to Lord's for their seventh one-day final, the same number as opponents Lancashire who had beaten Surrey by four runs in the other semi-final thanks mainly to 65 from veteran captain Clive Lloyd.

Having already used two captains during the season, Sussex very nearly had to employ a third for the final. A week before beating Worcestershire Gould injured his hand in a Championship game against Derbyshire at Eastbourne and on the final day handed the gloves to Reeve. It enabled Gould to take his first two wickets in first-class cricket as Sussex won with 11 balls to spare.

He quickly recovered but on 17th August, three weeks before the final, Gould tore hip muscles, aggravating an old injury, warming-up before a Sunday League match against Kent. He still scored 65 but afterwards was told he would be sidelined for at least ten days, possibly longer.

He said: "I had a terrible time. When I fell over I really thought I was going nowhere near the final. Even a week before it was touch and go and I felt really low. But I went to see a physio in Brighton and she gave me some real pain. It hurt like crazy but the next day it felt a bit better.

"The club was still concerned of course, so I went to play for Brighton Brunswick up in Surrey somewhere – Mitcham I think – and I got a few runs and the next day I woke up and was fine. It was always going to take something to stop me playing in a Lord's final. I was batting and keeping well at the time and enjoying the captaincy but for a few days it was touch and go."

Martin Speight took Gould's place in three Championship games including a drawn match against Nottinghamshire at Hove which preceded the final when Parker and Alan Wells both made confidence-boosting hundreds. Sussex did not have a game in the week leading up to Lord's but their preparation was the same apart from a session with a local gent's outfitters who had supplied the squad with pale blue suits for the big day.

There were no nets at Lord's on the eve of the game. Instead, after booking into their hotel a stone's throw from the ground, Gould took his players to his local pub, *The Pheasant* in Slough. He says: "We didn't over-do it or anything, just a couple of lagers to relax the boys. I could sense some of the younger ones were a bit on edge so it helped settle them down a bit."

If anyone was showing signs of nerves it was Gould, who recalls: "I'd booked an early-morning alarm call but by the time it came I had been awake for hours, just chewing over different scenarios in my mind such as what it would be like to score the winning runs or take the vital catch.

"I walked to the ground with our scorer Len Chandler. Len liked a bet like I did and he had a copy of the *Sporting Life*, which he always had at games. We must have talked about who'd win the 3.30pm at Redcar but it was my mind that was racing and the nearer we got to the ground the more of a sense of occasion I felt. There were hundreds of Sussex and Lancashire supporters there – in those days, of course, the September final at Lord's always sold out."

As usual at Lord's at that time of year there was moisture about and Gould debated with his players whether to bowl first – the norm in September finals – or bat on what looked a flat pitch. He was still weighing up his options when he strolled out to toss with Lancashire captain Clive Lloyd and realised Sussex had an advantage before a ball was bowled.

He said: "It was Clive's last game but they had a soppy moment because they picked him ahead of Patrick Patterson. They could only play one overseas player and they chose him on sentiment. We were delighted. Ray Alikhan was all ready to go out and take on Patterson, who was as quick as they came back then, and instead they opted for Clive."

Lloyd had just celebrated his 42nd birthday and had played fairly regularly for Lancashire that season in one-day cricket including a hundred in the Roses Match at Old Trafford back in May in the Benson & Hedges Cup.

"Clive was one of the nicest people I've met in the game and a great servant to Lancashire but he'd finished," says Gould. "His time was up and he hadn't played as much in the Championship because their bowling attack was poor. When we found out he was playing instead of Patterson the guys went 'Wow.' It definitely lifted the spirits."

Gould got out his lucky 2p coin and called correctly again and decided to bowl, but he was soon regretting his decision as Gehan Mendis, against the county he had left at the end of 1985, and Graeme Fowler posted 50 in 13 overs against Imran and le Roux.

"The worst we bowled was in the final," says Gould. "The wicket was green but I should have known better. It's just a good wicket at Lord's unless it's cloudy and that day it wasn't particularly overcast. I got it in my head that we needed to bowl because it was green and had a look of dampness.

"It nipped around early on but Garth didn't bowl as well as he could. He had never played in a Lord's final and froze. Tony Pigott froze and so did Adrian Jones and for a while we didn't have anywhere to go."

After completing an over le Roux made his way to the fine-leg boundary and a spectator threw him a blonde wig.

Gould says: "Garth was losing his hair and was a bit conscious about it but he stuck the wig on and we all turned around, saw it and started pissing ourselves with laughter. It just broke the ice a bit, we started to relax and things began to happen."

After a brief but expensive three-over spell by Jones, which cost 25 runs, Gould summoned Reeve to bowl in tandem with Colin Wells. Gould wasn't moving as well as he would have liked behind the stumps but he caught Fowler off Wells when the batsman chased width and then Reeve claimed the key wicket of Mendis, lbw for 17, to a ball which swung under the overcast skies. Gould says: "Mendo had left under a bit of a cloud and when Dermot knocked him over we gave him a bit of a send-off."

As Mendis departed the ground rose as one to acclaim the familiar figure of Lloyd, wearing his floppy white sun-hat, as he walked out to begin his penultimate innings as a professional cricketer (he finished his career in a John Player

League game at Bristol the following day). Gould had told his players beforehand to offer the great West Indian a guard of honour. It was, of course, the right thing to do but Gould had an ulterior motive, and recalls: "We thought it might distract him. Everyone in the ground were on their feet and you could tell Clive was genuinely moved by it."

Four minutes later Lloyd had done a Don Bradman – got a duck in between a standing ovation all the way to the wicket and another all the way back again after Reeve trapped him leg before third ball.

Gould says: "It was an absolute purler. It came back down the slope and rapped Clive on the shin. He was dead in front and slowly Kenny Palmer's finger came up. He probably didn't want to give it but he had too, it was so plumb. It was a massive moment in the game but I didn't run off and celebrate like a mad man. I thought 'let the man go off with a bit of dignity' and we all applauded him off the field."

Reeve picked up two more wickets – John Abrahams and Steve O'Shaughnessy – and when Lancashire were 112-5 after 40 overs the pre-match predictions that Sussex's attack would prove too strong looked to be coming true but then Neil Fairbrother and all-rounder Andy Hayhurst, counter-attacking against le Roux, put on 103 for the sixth wicket.

"They batted well but then Imran came back and bowled a magnificent spell at the end," remembers Gould. "He got Hayhurst and Chris Maynard out but the back had been broken by Dermot. Four for 20 in 12 overs with four maidens was outstanding bowling. But I still thought they got 50 runs more than they should have."

Maynard did strike Imran for three successive boundaries and in the last over Mike Watkinson lofted Tony Pigott for a straight six before Lancashire's innings closed on 242-8, the fifth highest in Lord's finals. Sussex would need to score at just over four runs an over on a pitch holding few terrors.

Instead of Patterson's fearsome pace Alikhan had to face the fast-medium Paul Allott and slightly slower Mike Watkinson instead. He was bowled by Allott for six but by the time Lancashire claimed their second success Sussex were on their way after a stand of 137 between Green and Parker as Sussex reached 117-1 at tea from 25 overs.

"They both batted beautifully," remembers their captain. "Paul had had a bit of a stop-start year but he was a class player. At the time there were a few people at the club who wanted him out but it would never have happened while I was there. He had so much pedigree and, of course, he was one of the best fielders in the country."

As Parker and Green blossomed so the choruses of Sussex by the Sea from their supporters in the Tavern Stand grew more vociferous.

Green was stumped for 62 but still finished as leading run-scorer in the competition with 202. Parker, who was suffering from cramp, was caught at long leg for 85 but batting conditions were now at their easiest and Imran Khan and Colin Wells put together an unbroken stand of 53, Wells winning the game with a six off Watkinson off the second ball of the 58th over. Sussex had won the competition for the fourth time by seven wickets, with Gould sitting on the balcony with his pads on secretly hoping he could have got out there to hit the winning runs.

Gould recalls: "Alan Wells was due in but I said I'd go next and he took it slightly the wrong way though in the event neither of us were needed. Until then Alan had had a slightly stop start career. There were a lot of people at the club who wanted him out and when I heard Middlesex were interested we rewarded him with a two-year contract and he became a very fine player. Colin played his part that day too. He seemed to blossom after 1986 and became a slightly more aggressive cricketer which I think suited him."

After Gould received the trophy in near darkness on the Lord's balcony – no stage on the outfield or presentation party in those days – the celebrations began. "The noise in the changing room afterwards was deafening," remembers Gould. Adrian Jones put his ghetto blaster on and played UB40's version of Red Red Wine which was rather appropriate because a lot of that was drunk over the next few hours."

Amazingly, Sussex were back in action the next day when a near full-house at Hove acclaimed the new cup winners before a John Player Sunday League game against Yorkshire. Nine of the cup-winning team (Speight and Phillipson came in for Alikhan and Imran) overcame hangovers to ease to victory by seven wickets before the players convened again to decide what to do with their share of the £19,000 NatWest prize money.

"It was a magical few days," says Gould, whose memory of 1986 is as clear as a bell 26 years on. "For me there was going back to Lord's and the county where I'd played a lot of my cricket and leading my team out in a major final. I know it sounds clichéd but I'd always dreamed of that and my dream came true. Wonderful, wonderful times."

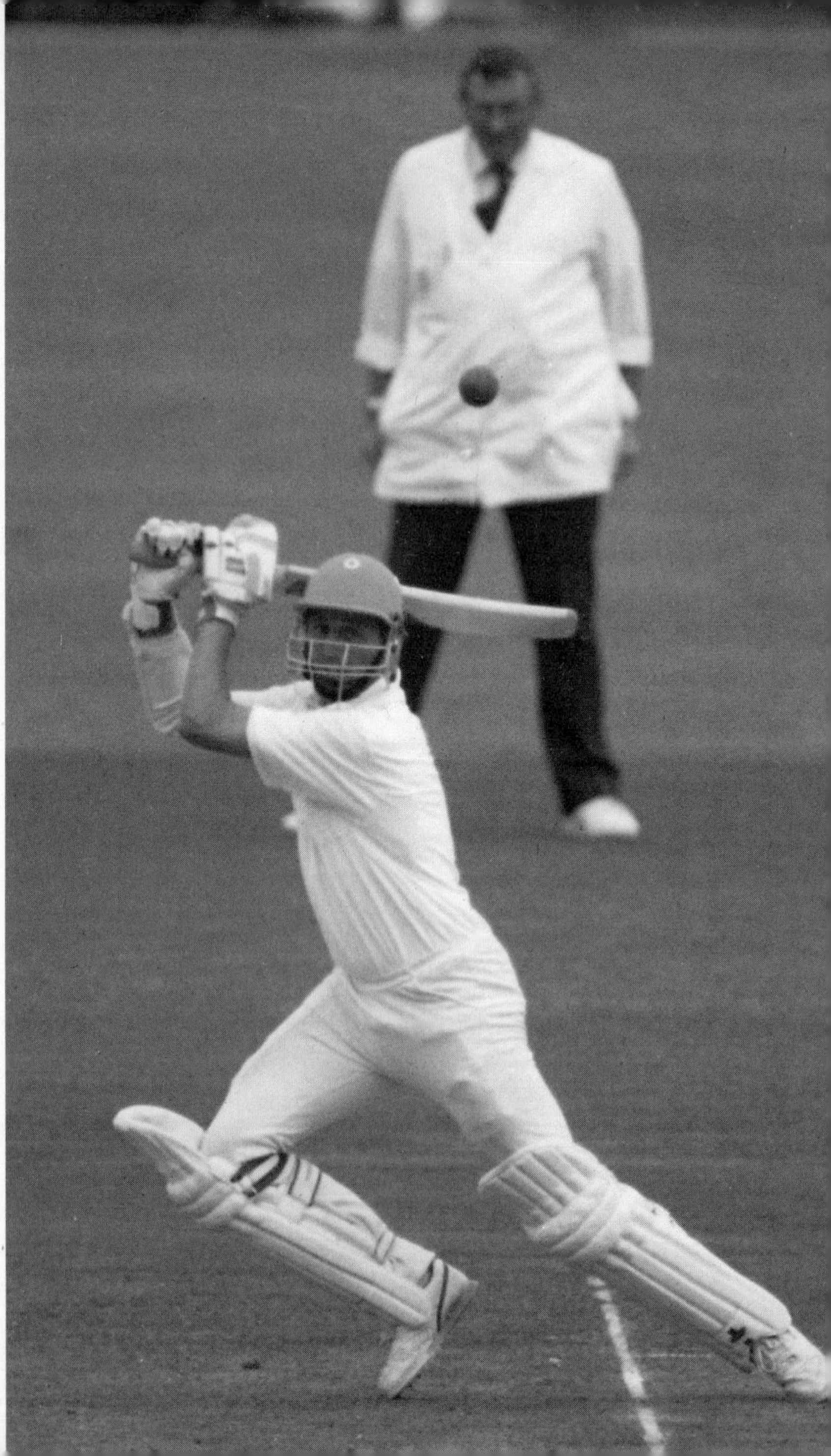

NEIL LENHAM

1993: Three Records – Three Defeats

IT'S NOT, NEIL Lenham smiles, necessarily one to tell the grandchildren. During a week in September 1993 the Sussex batsman scored 328 runs in four visits to the crease as part of a side which made 1,536 runs in three games – and lost the lot.

The defeats to Hampshire at Portsmouth, when both sides made 300 in a Sunday League game, and the run-feast at Hove in the Championship, when Essex scored 412 in 84 overs on the last day, have long been forgotten even though records were broken in both matches.

But memories of the 1993 NatWest final at Lord's still burn painfully in the minds of those who played in it, like Lenham, and the thousands of Sussex supporters who watched with amazement as their side failed to defend a total of 321 in a 60-over encounter and lost off the last ball.

That defeat to Warwickshire on 4th September 1993 – seven years after Lenham had been 12th man when Sussex beat Lancashire to win their last one-day title – prompted the gradual decline and eventual disintegration of a side which didn't achieve anywhere near as much as it should have done. Within four years only four of the finalists were still at Hove – Lenham, Bill Athey, Keith Greenfield and Peter Moores. The scars of that unbelievable afternoon, when Sussex seemed to be in control for 119 of the 120 overs, took a long time to heal.

For Lenham, the NatWest in 1993 represented the best of times and the worst of times. Lord's was the nadir of his and quite a few of his team-mates' careers but he does have happier memories of Sussex's run to the final and in particular the semi-final win against Glamorgan when he and skipper Alan Wells rescued a seemingly hopeless position to secure victory in the last over and deny Viv Richards a farewell appearance at headquarters in his final season in the game.

In a Sussex career which spanned 13 years Lenham scored more than 13,000 runs including 20 first-class hundreds and had it not been for injuries he might have played for England.

At Brighton College, he was regarded as one of the best schoolboy prospects in the country and captained England Schools. He should be remembered for a lot more than the distinctive canary-yellow helmet which he used to sport and which, when he first started wearing it, would cause opposition quick bowlers to suddenly find an extra yard of pace at the sheer effrontery of what he had on top of his head.

These days Lenham remains a familiar figure at Hove. After retiring in 1997 because of a persistent foot problem he joined the county's marketing department. After a decade behind the scenes he left Sussex to become Managing Director of Newbery, the Sussex-based cricket equipment manufacturers whose base is still at the County Ground.

"When you look at that side in 1993, which had been around for a few years, we ought to have been more successful," he says. "People like David Smith, Bill Athey, Franklyn Stephenson and Tony Pigott had all played international cricket. Alan Wells, Ian Salisbury and Ed Giddins went on to play for England as well.

"We did underachieve a little bit for a few years. We had a massively talented side and I'm not sure why we didn't achieve more. We played to win certainly and we played our cricket hard, but for whatever reason we didn't really click. One theory I have is that we might have done better if there had been two divisions back then. By the end of the season quite a lot of soft cricket could be played if there was nothing at stake. We needed to have a purpose. We were better when the stakes were high and the odds were against us."

Rather like 1986, but without the happy ending, Sussex had improved slowly as the 1993 season progressed. At the end of July they were second-bottom in the Championship but four wins from the last seven games lifted them to tenth and they only just failed to force victory in two of the other three matches.

In the Sunday League they came fourth, having led the table in mid-June after winning four and tying the other of their first five matches. They reached the quarter-finals of the Benson & Hedges Cup but Alan Wells and another potential match-winner Martin Speight were both run out and Lancashire beat them by five wickets with three overs to spare.

Like the team, Lenham's own form improved as the summer wore on. Over the years he suffered from more than his fair share of injuries. He lost count of the number of times he broke his fingers. It was an occupational hazard for opening batsmen of course, but it happened to him more than others. Fifteen years after he retired his hands still look as if they have just gone through a mangle. "It's not my best physical attribute," he smiles.

In 1993, though, the problem was his feet and it would eventually lead to his retirement. Lenham says: "I had snapped a tendon at the bottom of my foot a few years before and the other foot was kind of rebelling, to compensate if you like. I needed injections to play in both the semi-final and final in 1993. I soldiered on for another four years but it was so bad I could hardly walk some days. There just wasn't any point in carrying on."

Lenham didn't play in the first-round win over Wales, who were making their first appearance in the competition, at Hove on 22nd June. Smith was also absent but fellow opener Bill Athey made 92 and Keith Greenfield an unbeaten 96. With Wales 89-6 chasing a target of 258 Wells gave Greenfield and Athey seven overs apiece.

"Remember the games were 60 overs and quite often you needed a couple of guys to bowl the fill-in overs," says Lenham. "Keith bowled useful seam-up and he took what was probably the most crucial wicket of the season when he got Viv Richards out in the semi-final. I used to enjoy bowling. They used to hide me in the lower middle-order and I would sneak on and bowl five or six overs. I didn't tend to open in the one-day side because Ath and Smithy were a very good opening pair."

Proof of that came in the second round game, also at Hove, against a Hampshire side featuring Robin Smith, David Gower and Malcolm Marshall. Robin Smith's hundred on a good wicket helped take his side to 248-4 but Athey and David Smith made light work of that and had levelled the scores when Smith was yorked by Cardigan Connor for 123, leaving Speight to hit the winning runs. Athey scored 107 and their partnership was a new Sussex first-wicket record for the competition.

Lenham was fit again at the end of July but John North was still preferred to him for the quarter-final at Northampton, although North only made 11 runs batting at number six and did not bowl. The following day, Lenham made the first of two half-centuries in the Championship victory over Durham and regained his place in the one-day side the following week in the Sunday League win against Worcestershire.

Victory over a strong Northamptonshire side in their own back yard had imbued Wells and his players with the belief that they could go all the way. Sussex looked beaten when a rain-curtailed first day ended with the home side needing 85 off 20 overs with seven wickets in hand. But Allan Lamb, dropped on nought by Smith, was run out by Alan Wells for 71 and his side cracked under the pressure, losing seven wickets for 43 runs. "That was perhaps our best performance of the season," says Smith. "On the second day we came out and produced a team effort with as much drive and determination as I have ever seen. They were the holders and we steamrollered them to defeat by 40 runs. Franklyn and Ed Giddins bowled tremendously well and it was a very satisfying day."

Two days before the semi-final Lenham played in a Sunday League game at Hove against Worcestershire. He was part of the first one-day hat-trick by a Worcestershire player when Richard Illingworth had him stumped for nine and he bowled five wicket-less overs as first change for 37 runs, although he did take a wonderful boundary catch to dismiss Graeme Hick.

"It was just good to be playing again," he said. "The foot had caused me a lot of problems but I felt fine. Did I think I would play in the semi-final? Probably not although to be fair Ollie (North) hadn't done a great deal in the quarter-final win and when I took his place on the Sunday I knew I had a good chance."

Tuesday 10th August – semi-final day – dawned sunny and warm and well before the gates opened queues were snaking down Eaton Road including a considerable number of Glamorgan fans. It was certainly the draw Sussex wanted – at home and against the side considered the weakest of the four semi-finalists.

There was, though, the Richards factor to consider. The great West Indian had galvanised Glamorgan after joining them in 1990 and although he was not to enjoy the finale he wanted at Lord's in 1993 he did lead them to the Sunday League title that season.

A crowd of 5,500 had shoehorned themselves into the County Ground by the time Hugh Morris won the toss and decided to bat. The Glamorgan captain and Steve James gave their side a solid start with 54 when Lenham came on first change and trapped James leg before for 31.

"With my bowling a lot depended on how I felt on the day," says Lenham. "If I was fit and in decent rhythm – and I was that day – I could do a good job as the fifth bowler. The pitch was quite slow and both Keith Greenfield and I bowled that nagging length which can be difficult to get away at Hove. We chopped and changed and Alan would work out who was bowling okay. Keith and I bowled 16 overs between us and picked up three wickets and Keith, of course, got the one we all wanted."

Richards' father had recently passed away which gave him even more incentive to honour his memory by ending his career in a final at the home of cricket. He had moved on to 22 when Greenfield held one back slightly and the great man chipped back a simple return catch. "I was fortunate to play against some fine players but Viv was the most dominant batsman I ever came across," says Lenham. "He was the key man that day and he looked like he'd got in when Keith got him out. At that stage we felt really confident."

Franklyn Stephenson returned to the attack to pick up 3-25 from his 12 overs and although Matt Maynard held Glamorgan together with 84 Sussex fielded tigerishly and held their catches. A score of 220 looked about 20 runs light even allowing for the sluggishness of the pitch.

Sussex's seamers had bowled superbly – Stephenson and Pigott in particular – but if the pitch suited them it was tailor-made for the Glamorgan trio of Steve Watkin, Steve "Basil" Barwick and the Dutchman Roland Lefebvre.

"Watkin made a career out of bowling line and length, ball after ball, and in one-day cricket at that time there were few better bowlers than Basil," says Lenham. "Obviously there were a few nerves floating about as well and we didn't make the best of starts."

Sussex were soon 12-2 with Smith and Speight both out. "Roland Lefebvre bowled very well and Steve Watkin was very tight, getting me to drag one on for eight," remembers Smith. "I was lured into a rash shot because it wasn't easy out there, particularly for poor Billy Athey who was just blocking and blocking it while we got further behind the clock. It was in total contrast to Bill's knock with me against Hampshire but on this occasion it didn't help our cause at all."

Athey was eventually dismissed for 17 and while skipper Wells was beginning to blossom no one was able to stay with him as wickets fell regularly and Welsh voices grew louder.

When Peter Moores was sixth out Lenham and Wells had 15 overs left to double their score and win the game.

"I was due to come in at number five, but they sent Keith and Franklyn up the order to try and whack our way out of trouble but it backfired a bit," says Lenham. "Number eight was the lowest I ever batted and I think Glamorgan had forgotten about me a little bit. Alan was holding the fort and the plan was just to tick over and see where it took us."

Although Glamorgan's seamers had been consistent, off-spinner Robert Croft was proving relatively expensive, bowling nine wicket-less overs for 52. Richards came on to bowl his seam-up but his three overs conceded 25 runs and suddenly Sussex had momentum again.

"There was nothing wrong with the pitch," says Lenham. "It was slow but perfectly okay. I just thought some of our guys struggled with the occasion a bit. When I went in I had nothing to lose really and I think they definitely thought they had the game won. Scoring 100 runs in 15 overs is tough but we took on Croft and that got us back to needing six or seven runs an over and then we thought we had half a chance. They panicked at that stage and it worked in our favour."

Wells played what he regarded as his best one-day innings for Sussex. "Alan was a fine player," agrees Lenham. "He was organised, especially in one-day cricket. We ran well and he was a good man to bat with and we had some good partnerships. We had totally different techniques which seemed to work for us. He moved his body forwards on the front foot but could rock back and play off the back foot and I played mainly off the back foot. I would sit in and he would go at the ball."

David Smith, sitting in the dressing room, admits the rest of the side had regarded Sussex's chances of reaching the final as slim before the Wells-Lenham axis flourished. He says: "We'd almost given it up but Alan completed one of the best one-day hundreds you will see and Viv didn't get his goodbye final. He had stirred things up quite a bit on the field when we were batting by the way he was bulling around and making a lot of noise. He wound himself up just a bit too much."

Wisden described Wells' unbeaten 106 off 131 balls as "a brilliant one-day innings in which he manipulated the ball masterfully. Lenham, who finished with 47 from 43 balls, gave him excellent support". As the Welsh wilted and their fans fell silent, the game was won by three wickets with four balls to spare and Sussex had reached their first Lord's final for seven years.

It had been an intense occasion but the Sussex players still joined their vanquished opponents for a beer in Glamorgan's sea-front hotel later that evening. "A load of their supporters were there and seemed amazed to see us in there, not being able to understand how we could all have a drink together after such a tense semi-final," says Smith.

Sussex were now playing with a swagger. Two days after the semi-final Speight smashed 184 in a Championship game with Nottinghamshire while Lenham, promoted to number seven in the Sunday League match, made 28 at the end of the Sussex innings and then took a wicket as Sussex won by 94 runs.

Six days before Lord's Sussex travelled to Portsmouth for a Sunday League game and ended up losing despite scoring 312-8 in the days when matches were of 50 overs' duration.

Wells made another hundred and Lenham, up to the giddy heights of number five in the order, hit 69. But Hampshire won off the penultimate ball as the seven bowlers employed, including Lenham, suffered at the hands of Paul Terry and Robin Smith, who both made hundreds.

Sussex's preparations for the final involved a four-day Championship game against Essex at Hove which produced the highest aggregate for a first-class match in England as 1,808 runs were scored and only 20 wickets fell.

"In hindsight, Peter Eaton didn't do us a lot of favours that week," says Lenham. "It was an absolute shirt-front, you were at the stage of the season when bowlers were beginning to feel tired and if you got in it was pretty much a case of help yourself."

Seven players made hundreds, including North and Greenfield, with Lenham falling for 149 in the second innings after making a half-century in the first. On the last day Essex needed 411 to win in 92 overs and got there with eight overs to spare after John Stephenson and Nasser Hussain scored hundreds.

"It wasn't the ideal preparation because a few of our bowlers were very tired at the end of it and it was a quick turnaround," says Lenham. "We lost the game, got showered and changed and drove straight up to Lord's on the Friday evening."

The pre-match pressure was all on Warwickshire. The Bears were one of the wealthiest counties in the country but had won just two one-day trophies since their last Championship success in 1972. Bob Woolmer had just taken over as coach but they went into the final on the back of four Championship defeats which had seen them slump to third from bottom in the table. Their fast-bowling spearhead Allan

Donald was in Sri Lanka touring with South Africa and there were injury worries over their new-ball pair Tim Munton and Gladstone Small.

But they had two things in their favour. While Sussex headed to Lord's after four energy-sapping days against Essex Warwickshire had rested for most of the week. And there was also the Reeve factor.

In his two previous Lord's finals Dermot Reeve had been man of the match, first with Sussex against Lancashire in 1986 and then with Warwickshire three years later when he bowled 12 overs against Middlesex at a cost of 27 runs and scored 42 from number six as his side won a low-scoring game with two balls to spare.

Woolmer was convinced Reeve would again play a significant part. "He leads by example," he said on the eve of the final. "It's tough being an all-rounder in the modern game with counties playing five days straight. It's almost like playing a Test match, but he copes very well."

Lenham knew all too well what Reeve was capable of. "Dermot leaving Sussex definitely weakened us, certainly until Franklyn Stephenson was established as our all-rounder," he says. "He was an outstanding bowler when the ball did a bit, as it invariably did in September finals, and he hit in unorthodox areas. He was a thinking cricketer in a lot of ways."

Although Saturday 4th September dawned dry and bright there was moisture in the air and Warwickshire's decision to bowl after Reeve won the toss was no surprise. "We would have bowled because we knew it would nip around," says Lenham.

Athey fell with just four runs on the board but in many ways his departure did Sussex a favour. Martin Speight might not have been everyone's choice as the ideal player to come in when there was lateral movement, but he played an innings that set the tone for the day.

"Speighty decided there was only one way for it and that was to play his natural game," says Lenham. "He was a very talented young man and took the attack to them." As he came down the pitch to loft Munton and Small, who had both been declared fit, over the top a bemused Smith looked on at the other end.

"Martin played in the same way as he would a benefit match. There was one over from Gladstone when he played and missed at four balls because it wasn't easy but he kept going in his own merry way. When he swept, he nearly decapitated Asif Din at short leg and then he pulled a ball off the front foot from Munton which went miles.

"During one over he had scored nine off the first four balls and I went down the wicket and said 'it's pointless me saying that's alright for this over isn't it Sprog?' and he replied 'Yeah, it is really!' He hit the next ball for four!"

Speight scored 50 off 51 balls but Smith, using a bat Peter Eaton had repaired with glue and tape the previous week, matched him shot for shot in a stand of 103. Sussex briefly lost momentum with the wickets of Wells and Stephenson but the tempo picked up again when Lenham walked out in front of the 25,908 crowd to play one of the favourite innings of his career.

Lenham recalls: "I was nervous and to be honest if I hadn't been in a Lord's final something would have been wrong. It was the biggest game I'd played in but once I'd got myself established I didn't really pick up the noise of the crowd. The pitch flattened out, we were positive the whole way through and after the start Speighty had given us we knew we could aim for something in excess of 300.

"Smithy was great to bat with. In that era, when there were still some decent quicks around, you were going nowhere as a batsman if you didn't stand up for yourself. Smithy was a very brave player and his forte was definitely facing quick bowling. He played magnificently that day."

Smith, driving the ball with impressive authority, made 124. Not bad for a player whose participation in the final had been in doubt in the build-up to the game because of a persistent rib injury. But if Speight had taken the game to Warwickshire then Lenham did even better. *Wisden* called it "a depth charge of an innings" – 58 off 51 balls. "I remember going down the wicket to Neil and saying 'do you think we've got enough?' after we went past 300," says Smith. "It was meant to be a joke after we had scored 312 against Hampshire the previous Sunday and lost. We certainly didn't expect to go for 300 twice in a week."

Smith sacrificed his wicket going for a run off the final ball when Greenfield was on strike. He batted through the innings for 124 and could savour the adulation that Lenham had enjoyed earlier when he walked back through a packed Long Room to the changing room where Jamie Hall held the door open and Smith, who had lost six pounds during his innings, entered to wild acclaim from his team-mates.

"We ended up demoralising their bowlers," says Lenham. "Smithy played a wonderful innings and when I came in the situation was perfect for me. I could go for my shots because I knew we still had wickets in hand. We scored 83 off the last ten overs."

Sussex made 321-6.

While Smith had fluids poured down him to make sure he would be back on the field ten minutes later Wells made sure there was no complacency. "Alan said the right things and initially of course it all went well for us," says Lenham.

Warwickshire lost both openers with the score on 18 and at that stage there only looked to be one winner. Dominic Ostler was the third wicket to fall when he dragged a full toss from Ian Salisbury to Smith at mid-wicket with 93 on the board.

Then came the fightback. Paul Smith – "all long hair and long handle" according to *Wisden* – found an ally in Asif Din and either side of tea they added 71 in 15 overs. Sussex were haemorrhaging runs and Wells and his bowlers seemed powerless to prevent it. "Even when they were going well I don't think we thought we were going to lose but I kept looking up at the scoreboard and they seemed to be getting closer and closer," says Lenham. "Asif played the innings of his life that day but one or two things didn't go for us."

In particular, Stephenson clearly pulled the ball back inside the rope, even though he had one hand on it, yet third umpire Alan Whitehead signalled four. "It was the first time they'd used the third umpire in a final and it was a poor decision," says Lenham. "Of course it shouldn't have mattered but that saved run would have won us the game." Stephenson was even more forthright: "I'm not a cheat – I was not touching the ball, that decision cost us the game."

Smith was fourth out in the 36th over for 60 with the total on 164. Even then Din and new batsman Reeve needed to score at more than a run a ball. Wells delayed bringing on Greenfield and Lenham, who would have taken pace off the ball, while Pigott was leaking runs at seven an over.

"That was where we suffered because of that Essex game," says Lenham. "Our bowlers were tired, Lester more than most. In hindsight I could have bowled more and Keith maybe as well. We just didn't bowl well but you always felt if we could get either Asif or Dermot out we would still be OK."

The penultimate over started with Warwickshire needing 20 runs and although Reeve and Din had added 142 in 23 overs the light was fading fast. Cars travelling down St John's Wood Road had their headlamps on and the light above the scoreboard pierced the gathering gloom. Ed Giddins bowled a magnificent over, conceding just five runs and persuading Din to drive to deep cover where Speight took the catch. He had scored 104 from 106 balls.

Reeve was on strike when the final over, to be bowled by Stephenson, began with 15 runs needed. "You usually back yourselves nine times out of ten in that situation but Frankie was a bit nervous and Dermot was the best player to have in that situation," says Lenham. "He was always up for a challenge."

Stephenson offered the batsman too much width as his line deserted him and Reeve plundered 13 from the first five deliveries which left Roger Twose to face his first ball of the match needing to score two runs to bring his side an outrageous victory. Wells crowded his men around the bat including Smith, who decided to run at the batsman from silly point. "I thought if it hits me I'll be able to stop them running one," said Smith. Instead, Twose sliced the ball over the infield and over Lenham's head at short third man and set off to complete the two runs required.

"You have to give them credit because they kept punching even when all seemed lost. Of course we would all have done things differently given the opportunity," says Lenham. "I remember Smith offering a chance quite early in his innings but Alan was conscious that Frankie might collide with him at mid-on and it went down. Dermot (81 not out) played the innings of his life and got a new contract as a result of it. We were in shock afterwards. Not a lot was said because what can you say in that situation? We were in charge of that game until the last over really."

The press hailed it as the greatest one-day final ever but cold analysis suggests it wasn't quite the feast everyone regarded it as at the time. The five England Test bowlers on show disappeared for 331 runs off 55 overs and there were 31 wides and 22 no balls. Warwickshire donated 45 extras, Sussex 35.

As he reflects nearly 20 years later on those two matches – the semi-final and final – Lenham retains a sense of pride for the part he played but he agrees that Lord's 1993 marked the beginning of the end for a group of players who should have achieved far more than they did.

"Alan was a fine captain who had a side that should have done better than it did," he says. "Sometimes we didn't quite click but when we did we destroyed the opposition. The committee at the time always seemed very supportive and I never had any problems but when Alan lost the captaincy in 1997 it all went downhill very quickly."

In fact the decline started before that. In 1994 Sussex lost in the early rounds of both one-day competitions and won just five Sunday League games. Halfway through the 1995 season coach Norman Gifford lost his job and the following year Wells had gone too, holding a press conference about his departure in the garden of his local pub in Berwick, East Sussex.

The rebirth of the club, first under Peter Moores and then Chris Adams, culminated in a first Championship a decade after the Lord's debacle. By then Lenham was part of the administration at Sussex but he recognised how much the cricketing landscape at Hove had changed.

Lenham says: "When we lost all the capped players in 1997 we knew it would be tough and it was. I retired that year and the side had some good youngsters coming through and a few old sweats like myself, Ath, Mooresy himself and Mark Robinson. I remember we got to the semi-final of the NatWest but Warwickshire were all over us at Edgbaston and beat us easily.

"Their good years under Woolmer and Dermot stemmed from winning that final and they dominated domestic cricket for the next few years. We went backwards but it was still very special to be involved when we did finally start to get things right.

"Of course I'd loved to have won a trophy while I was playing but it wasn't to be. I still had a wonderful career though and I did play in a Lord's final and back then that did mean something. 1993 seems a long time ago but people still bring it up. It was a great game to play in. I only wish we'd won the bloody thing!"

BIBLIOGRAPHY

Ranji by Alan Ross (Collins)

Ranji: The Strange Genius of Ranjitsinhji by Simon Wilde (Aurum Press)

The Family Fortune (A Saga of Sussex Cricket) by Alan Hill (Scan Books)

Young Jim – The Jim Parks Story by Derek Watts (Tempus)

Sussex Cricket by John Marshall (Heinemann)

Cricket Rebel by John Snow (Hamlyn Books)

Sussex Cricket by Sir Home Gordon (Convoy Books)

Larger Than Life by David Smith (with Paul Newman) (Two Heads Publishing)

From The Sea End by Christopher Lee (Partridge Press)

The Year of the Magical Martlets by Nicholas Sharp

Good Old Sussex by the Sea by Nicholas Sharp

The Longest Journey by Paul Weaver and Bruce Talbot (Sutton Publishing)

The Flight of the Marlets (The Golden Age of Sussex Cricket) by Paul Weaver and Bruce Talbot (Breedon Books)

100 Sussex Greats by John Wallace (Tempus)

Hedley Verity: Portrait of a Cricketer by Alan Hill (Mainstream Publishing)

Plus assorted *Wisdens, Playfairs* and Sussex CCC handbooks.

I have also consulted archive copies of the *Brighton Argus, Sussex Daily News* and *Daily Express*